Autism in Adults

Dr Luke Beardon has worked for decades in a wide range of roles in the field of autism, and has won many autism-related awards. He describes his interests as 'anything relating to autism' and has a passion for the rights and equalities of autistic children and adults. His current role is Senior Lecturer in Autism at The Autism Centre which is part of Sheffield Hallam University's Institute of Education.

Overcoming Common Problems Series

Selected titles

A full list of titles is available from Sheldon Press on our website at
www.sheldonpress.co.uk

Lists of titles in the Mindful Way and Sheldon Short Guides series are also available from Sheldon Press.

Overcoming Common Problems

Autism in Adults

DR LUKE BEARDON

This edition published by Sheldon Press in 2021

First published by Sheldon Press in 2017
An imprint of John Murray Press
A division of Hodder & Stoughton Ltd,
An Hachette UK company

9

A CIP catalogue record for this title is available from the British Library

Trade Paperback ISBN 9781529375411
eBook ISBN 9781529375428

Typeset by KnowledgeWorks Global Ltd.

Printed and bound in Great Britain by Clays Ltd, Elcograf S.p.A.

John Murray Press policy is to use papers that are natural, renewable and recyclable products and made from wood grown in sustainable forests. The logging and manufacturing processes are expected to conform to the environmental regulations of the country of origin.

John Murray Press
Carmelite House
50 Victoria Embankment
London EC4Y 0DZ

www.sheldonpress.co.uk

*To all the autistic people and their families
who have shared their lives with me; you're the real teachers.
And, as always, to my own family – without you, I am nothing*

Contents

Acknowledgements

There is a plethora of individuals to whom I owe a debt of gratitude, for varying reasons that need not be aired in public. I hope you know what you mean to me. In no particular order: Dr Nick Chown, Dr Sandra Beale-Ellis (and Joe), Julia Leatherland and family, my trimigo Piggy-Paws (and husband), Dr Linda Buchan and the Axia family, including Dream, Dean Beadle, Sarah Hendrickx, Kleio Cossburn and Caroline Lear. Last but never least, Ash – my ongoing dose of reality.

The first part of the section on 'Social anxiety' in Chapter 3 is an expanded version of my blog post 'Mustn't Grumble'.

1

Introduction – where I'm coming from

Never believe *anything* you read about autism.

Perhaps this statement requires some justification. After all, if you have bought this book you may well be somewhat disappointed at such an opening remark; if you are in a shop trying to decide whether to buy it or not, then it may well put you off!

There is no such thing as a 'typical autistic person'. There is extraordinarily little that can be said to be 'true' or 'valid' when pertaining to the whole of the population described as autistic. There is no 'one size fits all' approach, nor any description of an autistic person that will be true for all individuals. There are very few 'facts' about autism that are common to all individuals, and precious little advice that can be beneficial to all families, individuals, parents or professionals. Thus, everything you read or hear about autism, see on the TV, etc., must be taken with a very clear understanding that it may not be particularly relevant to you. The heterogeneity of the autistic population is such that there will be differences from one individual to the next, and what is of huge relevance to one party may have no meaning whatsoever to another. It is hugely frustrating to read suggestions that 'the best thing for children with autism is . . .' – or any similar definitive sentiment. What may work well for one individual could be a disaster for another. Taking this a stage further, what may work well for one individual one day could be a disaster for the same individual the next day. Such is the nature of autism.

By far the best approach (in my opinion) is that of unadulterated honesty. There will be nothing written in this book that I do not honestly believe; there may be some matters that I deliberately leave open ended, if there is no clear 'answer'. To constantly question the validity of what is being written, and the theories and perspectives that can be found 'out there', is good practice. But to digest the written word without question, and then to make the assumption that all that has been digested will be of relevance to your situation, goes against the principles of this book, and I would urge you not to take that route.

Let me say a bit about the perspective from which I'm writing. My understanding of autism has come about from decades of working in autism-related fields. I have been a support worker, an outreach worker, a service co-ordinator, a project officer, a development officer, an autism consultant, a trainer, a researcher and a lecturer – all within the autism field. I am lucky enough to have chatted at length about autism with hundreds of individuals on what is often known as the spectrum, as well as parents, carers, professionals and academics. I also have several personal connections within the field. My writing therefore stems from an amalgamation of experience, learning from others, research and almost constant rumination; I do not claim to be an expert on the subject, and anyone who does is misguided (one may have a high level of expertise in the field – but that does not mean one is an expert in all things related to autism). I do hope, though, that what I have written here will stimulate thought and be of help.

What is needed when reading about autism, hearing people talk about it, or listening to personal accounts, is a conscious process of questioning and translating. The questioning relates to the rationale behind the words, the potential validity, whether or not what is being said sounds reasonable. The translating is more problematic, but perhaps of considerably more value. Translation relates to the process of taking the relevant information and making it personal – to you, your child or teenager, your employee, your parent – whoever it is that you are reading this for in the first instance. Taking essentially generic material (however specific to autism) and applying it to a given situation is crucial if one is to get the most out of the literature, the speaker, and so on. The ability to read an autobiographical account and recognize which aspects are useful and which are less relevant is a wonderful skill to have. Reading a book written by a professional and having the ability to extract meaningful material and then apply it to a given individual is an ability worth nurturing. And all it requires, really, is a little thought. A simple but effective skill – thinking.

Putting this into practice is not, however, as easy as it may sound. True reflective thought is not a commonplace activity – nor is self-reflection when related to understanding of one's own thinking, behaving and communicating. Such introspection, however, is vital when engaging both with autistic people and with the literature pertaining to them. In other words, it is crucial to have a level of thought when engaging with autistic children and adults so as to ensure that you do not unwittingly engage in bad practice; similarly, it is important to ensure that when you are reading about autism you are not unwittingly digesting poor and/or inaccurate information. While this may seem onerous and time consuming, it is simply a fact of life; if we are not prepared to engage at the deepest level with an understanding of autism and then use our understanding to engage with the autistic population, then we must accept that we may be putting people with autism at a grave disadvantage.

Lack of understanding, and/or the lack of ability to apply good practice, will lead directly, in most cases, to damage to the individual and beyond. It is crucial that the general level of understanding of autism among professionals is as high as possible in order to reduce that risk. It is my aim to try and provide a set of words that will enable better understanding.

Everything that has been written here has a rationale. Some of it is based on research, some on experience; much of it is based on what the autism community have communicated to me, directly or indirectly. I do not claim that it is all 'true' – as you will see, a constant theme running throughout the autism literature is that there is very little that can be said to be 'true' – but everything will have a rationale. This rationale is always up for debate, of course, but I aim to be as clear as possible. To avoid narrative interruption I will try not to constantly write 'in my opinion' etc. – but of course, everything I write *will* be my opinion.

Terms and conditions

In this book, *I* means me, the author.
We is society in general.
You pertains to autistic readers.

There is a plethora of terms within the autism field that purport to 'describe' the autistic individual. Here are just some of them (in no particular order):

- autism
- Asperger syndrome (or Asperger's syndrome)
- Kanner's autism (or classic autism)
- autism spectrum disorder
- autism spectrum condition
- aspie
- on the autism spectrum.

The autistic person is a person who is autistic. Whether this should be what defines any individual is very much dependent on that individual him- or herself; certainly, being autistic will play a huge part in influencing that person's being simply because it is neurologically his or her cognitive style. Who is to say whether autism plays a bigger part than the myriad of other factors that influence human beings? Again, it will differ from one person to the next. Am I a person with tattoos, or a tattooed person? It doesn't really matter one way or the other, but I certainly should not be *defined* solely in this way. Am I often *described* as such by those wishing to latch on to an obvious (for the most part) aspect of me? Most likely, yes. It would be ridiculous of me to be offended in any way; I am, after all, someone who has tattoos. It is when people start to *judge* based on how one is described or how one presents that the offence is committed. To judge people in any way because they are autistic – that is the offensive act. To make assumptions simply because someone has a diagnosis of autism is where one goes astray. To be absolutely clear here, I am not making any connection between having tattoos (which is usually a choice) and being autistic. I am simply using tattoos as the analogy, in that one should *never* judge a person because he or she has a tattoo, in the same way that one should *never* judge a person because he or she is autistic.

The most recent research, conducted by psychologist Professor Elizabeth Pellicano in 2014, suggests that within the autism community the preferred option when identifying someone with autism is to refer to the person as 'on the autism spectrum' – however, individuals often prefer the term 'autistic' when describing themselves.

And yet, some would argue that 'person with autism' is preferable to any other term. There is much debate over whether 'person with autism' is problematic in relation to 'autistic person', and this is an instance of the whole 'person first' language debate.

The basis of the argument is that 'autistic person' suggests that autism is an intrinsic aspect of a persona, but that 'person with autism' implies that the person is an individual first and that the autism is somehow secondary, or an 'add-on' – which from my perspective is clearly not apt. However, both arguments can be embraced for different reasons; some may feel that autism is so much a part of who they are, of their very identity, that anything other than 'autistic' would be meaningless; others may feel that the fact they are autistic is almost incidental to how they identify themselves. For some, it simply comes down to preferred linguistic style.

The reality is that the arguments can be incredibly important for a significant proportion of the population, but for many it comes down to individual preference. Those who do feel strongly about it tend to feel *very* strongly about it; others are more ambivalent. Within this text I will use both terms; I believe that autism *is* an intrinsic aspect of a persona – but I also believe that the impact of being autistic can (and does) change quite dramatically dependent on the environment (this does *not* mean that I believe a person's autism will change – just its impact).

In terms of which phrase to use on an individual level within practice, it's perfectly appropriate to simply ask the individual or parent which term they prefer. What is not acceptable is to impose one's own view on an individual for whom it should be a personal choice. It is the individual's prerogative to describe him- or herself in terms which suit that individual.

Autism or Asperger syndrome? High-functioning autism? Or what?

The next aspect of terminology I want to deal with is that which refers to the various diagnostic terms that litter the textbooks and diagnostic manuals. Let's take the easiest first – you will not see autistic spectrum disorder, autism spectrum disorder, or autism condition used within this book. Autism is categorically *not* a disorder or condition, in my view, so those terms are out. I have also tended not to use the term Asperger syndrome (AS), despite its common usage. This must in no way detract from the sense of identity that people with AS will have with the term itself, but in essence I believe that the term autism can be used perfectly adequately to cover people with AS. This is hugely problematic as a result of history; historically, AS has come to be viewed as autism, but without an associated intellectual learning disability (there are all sorts of technicalities here, and many papers written about the perceived differences between autism and AS).

The idea that 'people with AS have average or above average intelligence' is one that has often bemused me. I am perfectly happy to accept it as a valid concept, but am concerned about the implication – that in relative terms, people with a diagnosis of autism as opposed to AS *do not* or *cannot* have average or above average intelligence. As far as I am aware, there is nothing to suggest that autistic people are any less intelligent than anyone else. In reality, what appears to have happened is that those who have a *co-morbidity with a learning disability* end up with the diagnosis of autism, and those without end up with the diagnosis of AS. This is misleading – autism, with no co-morbidity (i.e. without an additional, or co-morbid, mental health issue or learning disability), has nothing whatsoever to do with levels of intellectual ability, as many of my autistic doctoral students will attest.

High-functioning autism (HFA) is another term rife with ambiguity – or even inaccuracy. Experience shows that many people who have been given the diagnosis of HFA are, in reality, far from being 'high functioning'; intellectually there may be clear evidence of functioning at a high level in demographic terms, but this does *not* mean that the individual does not require support. In some cases individuals deemed 'high functioning' require very high levels of support, ironically enough to enable them to 'function' on a day-to-day basis.

Learning disability or learning difficulty?

While I'm on this subject, let's clear up the terms *learning disability* and *learning difficulty*. What follows is simply my version, for the purposes of clarity. For too long learning disability and learning difficulty have been used synonymously – which only ends up confusing the issues. Accuracy of terminology can be extremely important, simply so that all parties have a mutual understanding of what is being referred to. A learning disability can be viewed in a rather medical manner as an intellectual impairment; somewhat crudely (but out of necessity) this will often refer to an IQ level within a certain range (e.g. below 70). A learning difficulty, on the other hand, does not relate to intellectual ability at all, but to learning: a useful definition could be 'anything that reduces learning opportunities based on the way in which we teach'. So, to use the simplest example, a dyslexic student may well be intelligent, but may struggle to learn in the traditional learning environment. The latter part of the definition is crucial – if the same student is taught in a different manner, and is supported in the most effective way, his or her level of difficulty in learning may well decrease. Such students are equally dyslexic, but the impact of the dyslexia has been reduced. Similarly, I would suggest that autism is a learning difficulty – but the impact of autism can be considerably influenced by how the individual is supported.

The potential way forward

Going back to autism/AS, and the rationale behind 'merging' those terms; the most basic (and possibly the strongest) argument for this is that, given that all people with autism are individuals, any sub-categorization could be seen as an erroneous attempt to homogenize a heterogeneous population. Admittedly, the global term 'autism' itself could be seen to do this, but I will cover that elsewhere. The propensity to sub-categorize is not always helpful; the plethora of terms that are used to refer to people with autism seems to confuse rather than illuminate – and, worse, lead professionals to become over-reliant on the diagnostic term rather than the individuality of the person: all the debates over whether the term should be HFA or

AS, for example. My argument is that until there is absolute consistency in the understanding of what the difference is (supposing that there actually is one), there is little use in differentiating between the terms. This is not to suggest that two people, one with a diagnosis of HFA and the other with AS, cannot be extremely different individuals – of course they can. So, however, can two people both with a diagnosis of AS. As there is currently a total lack of consistency between the usage of the terms and what they actually mean, what is the purpose of the different terms?

Consider the following: two people are being referred to someone (in any capacity – as a teacher, friend, professional, etc.), one with a diagnosis of AS, the other with a diagnosis of HFA. Does that person, honestly, now know how to support those individuals differently? I suspect that the answer is no – he or she would have to meet the individuals before coming to any such decision. So this begs the question: just how useful is it to have these two different terms?

I believe that the term autism should be used to cover all individuals who are autistic. In doing so, one would be forced then to ascertain specifically how autism affects each individual (at that time, within that environment), rather than making assumptions related to the term itself. Of course, the problem – in the short term at least – is that for many people the term autism has negative connotations, and leads to all sorts of fallacious assumptions. Should this be a good enough reason to then alter the term or sub-categorize – or would a more profitable and useful way forward be the reduction of ignorance surrounding autism and the development of a better global understanding? I believe that the more individuals who are identified as autistic, the more people will realize how diverse the population actually is; in doing so, along with gaining a better understanding of autism, the general public will stop making assumptions based on limited knowledge, and begin to realize that it is unfeasible to make accurate suppositions about an individual simply because he or she is autistic.

Lastly, in this chapter, while the book includes much information related to adults, there are many principles and ideas that relate just as well to children and teenagers. So please feel free to think about the younger generation as well as the adult population while you read. Any examples of real-life situations are used with the permission of the individual concerned; for purposes of confidentiality, all names have been changed.

A note on the title

The 'in adults' component of the title needs some explanation. Autism is from birth to the end. And my view is that being autistic is intrinsic to the individual – not an 'add-on' or some thing in addition to the person. The 'in' part of 'in adults' refers to the subject matter discussed in the book, which is of relevance mainly (though not exclusively) to autistic adults; it is not intended to refer to autism being 'in' adults.

2

What autism isn't
(and a bit of what it is)

In this chapter I shall be identifying some of the myths (or misnomers) that have been associated with autism – and that in some cases are still associated with autism. I am not suggesting that certain aspects of the theory are specifically wrong, or that they are in no way useful in terms of understanding autism. Rather, it is a critique of their value when it comes to universality. In other words, no one theory fits all autistic people.

The autism spectrum

It is current practice to use the term 'spectrum' when referring to autism. The term is excellent in that it denotes the heterogeneity of the autism population, but problematic when it is translated to mean a spectrum from mild to severe. To suggest that one person's autism is more or less severe than another's according to some kind of grading system is not only fraught with problems, it can also be hugely offensive to the individual. The current DSM-5 (*Diagnostic and Statistical Manual* of the American Psychiatric Association, which sets out so-called autism diagnostic criteria) suggests that autism should be graded in relation to the levels of support the individual requires. This is far too simplistic. What might be required in terms of support for an individual in one environment will differ, often considerably, from what may be required in another. Some people may not need any support at all in many environments, but need extremely high levels of support in a minority of situations. Some might go for years without the need for support, but experience periods of (for example) weeks during which support is required constantly. Some might not need support simply because they have a job that suits them, a partner who understands them, and the perfect lifestyle for their needs – but if any element of this changes then the level of support they require may alter considerably. The person is equally autistic in any of the above scenarios, but the *impact* of the autism will differ from one environment to the next – and, in many cases, the difference will be extreme. Therefore, how can levels of support genuinely be determined? Or, to put it another way, how can autism genuinely be 'graded'? The argument rolls on . . .

What about the notion of severity? Again, I suggest that this can cause all sorts of problems, not least in relation to society's conceptual understanding of autism. A term such as 'severe autism' has long since been a part of general parlance, but what does it actually mean? Can one person's autism really be accurately identified as more severe than another's? In contrast, if severe autism exists then logically there must be . . . what? Neutral autism? Mediocre autism? Middle-of-the-road autism? And then – at the other end of the scale – the dreaded 'mild autism'? Being just a teeny bit autistic? Hardly autistic at all? Just having a cheeky splash of autism? (For clarification, the last few sentences include an element of sarcasm!)

These are *not* helpful notions – in fact, they can be extremely damaging. If one accepts that the individual is either autistic or not, then my view is to leave it at that, without trying to judge what sort of 'level' an individual might be at. I don't think it's that valid anyway. For me, what is of essential importance is the *impact that being autistic has on a person at any given time*. This can range from horrifically negative right through to sublimely positive – and sometimes both can be found *in the same individual*. So, if this dramatic difference can be seen at different times in the same person – what 'grade' is that person? Clearly, this is where the whole notion of 'autism severity' crumbles.

However, going back to my point that the concept of severity (positive and/or negative) could – and should – be applied *in context*, all of a sudden a useful model can be applied. This is entirely based on the following principle – and one which I believe is of the utmost importance:

AUTISM + ENVIRONMENT = OUTCOME

In other words, it is the combination of you, the autistic person, and the environment in which you find yourself that determines what sort of impact and outcome you will experience. Consider the following scenario:

> She entered the room; it had no electric light, but was beautifully lit with candles – unscented ones which didn't offend her olfactory sense. The room was a perfect square, with no pictures adorning the walls, and the simple desk had a single monitor that was sensibly aligned with the keyboard, so all lines appeared either parallel or perpendicular – just how she liked it. She was alone – alone to gather her thoughts, fiddle without fear of reprisal with the toys she had brought with her, no one to ask her difficult questions, no one to interrupt her thought processes. On the desk was a single sheet of paper, as expected, as was always the case on a working day. As always, there was a neatly printed list of instructions for her to follow to ensure that she completed her tasks on time, and the order in which they needed to be done. She spun quietly for a while, a huge smile on her face as she looked forward to another productive day at the office.

Now compare it with this one:

> She entered the room; instantly she was blinded by the harsh lighting, and her ears picked up the intense buzzing of electricity. Her senses were under attack – pictures hung askew, plug sockets which were turned on even though they had no plugs, the smell of stale coffee, the deafening din of people chatting – it all came at once to a point of near meltdown. She automatically went to her pocket to grab a toy to counteract her distress, only to remember her line manager had berated her the previous week for behaving immaturely. A colleague brushed past her – a double whammy, as not only did the personal contact make her skin scream, but the colleague also asked her how her weekend had gone, and she had been struck mute by the sensory overload, and now knew she must appear terribly rude for not answering. She is effectively blind and mute; she can't see where her desk is amid all the chaos, and she can't ask for help. Everyone else is sitting at their desks ready to be productive. She flees from the room, she has no choice. Yet another job down the toilet.

Bearing in mind that the above scenarios were written about the same person, it's easy to understand just how impactful the environment can be for the autistic adult – and how the outcome can be so very different. In the first scenario, the autism-friendly environment (including the absence of people) 'allows' the woman to be a positive, productive worker (this is simply an example that suits this person – I am not suggesting that all work environments need to be devoid of people to suit all autistic employees). In the latter, the lack of acknowledgement of autistic need means that she walks out of her job.

While this has been written in relation to a working environment, I believe that the same model can be applied across the span of your whole existence. The concept that I embrace is that autism itself could and should not be categorized in terms of severity, but that we should understand that outcomes for autistic adults will be hugely dependent on the environments we expose them to.

As a last word on the subject of grading – as mentioned a while ago – what does a label of 'mild autism' say to a person? I know very many people who have been told that they 'must only be mild' – though based on what evidence these remarks have been made I have no idea. Almost all (if not all) of the people I know who have been told their autism is 'mild' are severely affected every day – often, ironically enough, as a direct result of being perceived as mild! This can have a serious impact on mental health. If you are told you are mild, and yet you struggle from day to day, this can give you the impression that you are somehow not managing life very well; after all, if you're only mild then you should be OK with just a bit of effort. If, in fact, you are not managing at all well, where does that leave you in terms of your self-esteem? The label 'mild', in my view, should *never* be used in relation to autism.

'We're all a bit autistic'

No, we're not! I genuinely believe that one is either autistic or one is not. I accept that identifying whether you are autistic or not can be hugely problematic – but logic dictates that if one can be of only a single neurotype (autism being a specific neurological state), then one cannot be both autistic and non-autistic at the same time.

Certainly both populations will share similar 'traits' or characteristics – but so what? Making the immense, erroneous leap between acknowledging that both populations share the same 'trait' and subsequently assuming it means they share the same neurology is baffling in the extreme. Some may argue that there is a spectrum of humanity and that we are all on it together, which I can absolutely accept. However, we are at the same time all individual human beings, which I also accept. How, then, can we label populations as one thing or another – in this case, autistic, or not? And is it even helpful? My view is that we absolutely *can* define populations by neurotype. It is extremely helpful (or has the potential to be), and though they share all sorts of behavioural traits there is a clear difference between the autistic brain and the predominant neurotype (PNT) brain.

Lack of empathy

People with autism do *not* invariably lack empathy. Autism is not a state of being that has stemmed from being non-empathic. Plenty of autistic people are highly empathic. Some may consider themselves 'over-empathic'. The issue here is that there are a myriad of differing cognitive styles in the global population, and a plethora of differing experiences of living. Combined with the fact that empathy itself is not easily defined (i.e. there are different types of empathy), this means that it is far too simplistic to declare that people with autism lack empathy. Whole books have been written about this – but, in brief, it might be useful to take the following into consideration:

- the difference between shared experience and emotional intuitive empathy;
- the difference between intuitive and learned empathy;
- cross-neurological empathy.

The difference between shared experience and emotional intuitive empathy

If two people share a similar experience and have a similar emotional reaction, then they could be said to have empathy with one another within this context. For example, one individual might be able to empathize to a very high degree with someone else who has a fear of dogs after having been bitten by a dog as a child. A third party, on the other hand, who has only ever had positive experiences with dogs, might find it qualitatively more difficult to relate to this negative emotional state regarding dogs. The third person might *understand* at an intellectual level – but not necessarily empathize in terms of *feeling* the same way.

The 'shared experience' type of empathy is further complicated when autism is brought into the mix. How an autistic person reacts on an emotional level might differ considerably from a PNT who has gone through a similar experience. So, while two people may be able to empathize with one another if they have shared experiences, it cannot be assumed that this is the case if one individual reacts differently from the other at an emotional level.

'Shared experience' empathy is not the same as an intuitive understanding of the emotional states of others. The latter may have very little to do with having experienced similar events; rather, it is rooted in having a similar cognitive state and being able to imagine and understand what the other person may be experiencing, feeling or thinking – without conscious effort or even direct communication. I think it is very sensible to put forward the supposition that the more different the cognitive processes between any two individuals, the less likely high levels of intuitive emotional empathy will be.

The difference between intuitive and learned empathy

So – as noted above – there is intuitive empathy, which does not require any conscious thought or effort. But there is also learned empathy – where an individual might *work out* what another person is thinking or feeling, leading to a similar 'result' in terms of understanding compared to intuitive empathy. Many adults with autism will have had to spend much of their lives trying to 'work others out' – with differing degrees of success – and this is an example of learned empathy. Having learnt how to understand others does not make an autistic person any less autistic, but it may be a skill that goes some way towards masking autism, or leading people to think that one might not be autistic. The irony might be that the considerable effort made by the autistic adult in continuously working others out actually leads them to assume that intuitive empathy is not a problem, when the reality might be anything but.

Cross-neurological empathy

Dr Damian Milton refers to this as the 'double-empathy' problem. I refer to it as cross-neurological theory of mind (theory of mind is the ability to attribute mental and emotional states, such as beliefs, to oneself and others, and to subsequently understand that some beliefs will differ between oneself and others). In essence, what we are both suggesting is that it's not valid to suggest that people with autism lack a theory of mind – but that there is a lack of theory of mind across all neurological states. In other words it may well be the case that autistic individuals might have problems with understanding the thoughts, feelings, beliefs and behaviours of the PNT – but it is equally the case that the PNT will have difficulties in understanding the thoughts, feelings, beliefs and behaviours of the autistic individual.

Conversely, there may be high levels of empathy between autistic individuals; some will suggest that, in fact, their levels of empathy far outweigh what is commonly found within the general population. Certainly there are examples of intense empathic feelings for other people that demonstrate extraordinarily well developed theory of mind – sometimes autistic individuals will feel intensely on behalf of a person they don't know well, or even at all. There are also plenty of examples of intense empathic feeling for animals – which is another story altogether, but worth bearing in mind.

Autistic people lack social skills

This is simply not true. What is more likely to be a valid statement is 'autistic people lack the intuitive ability to understand unwritten PNT social rules' – which is a very different statement to make. To suggest that an autistic person is impaired in social skills is simplistic and very unfair – the inference is that the PNT social way of being is superior to the autistic social way of being, and that if the PNT way is not understood or followed then the autistic individual is at fault. If one were to take a different view – and understand that

to be autistic is to be part of a minority group – then one might conclude that while autistic people may be hugely disadvantaged by
not understanding PNT social rules, they are certainly not impaired.
I shall undertake a more in-depth exploration of social interaction
in Chapter 3.

So what is autism?

I absolutely do not subscribe to the medical model of autism (i.e.
that being autistic means that there is something 'wrong' with
you, and that there are 'impairments' that need 'fixing') – though,
equally, I accept that autism can cause lifelong serious problems for
some individuals and families. I am categorically not dismissing
those issues; however, it is not accurate to suggest that *all* autistic
individuals can or should be viewed according to a medical model.
The medical model identifies autism as a deficit – something to
be fixed, cured, or changed for the better. The social model, on
the other hand, implies that any problem that a 'disabled' person
might have is rooted in the environment – i.e. within society – and
that changes and adaptations within society will reduce or elim-
inate the negative issues faced.

Much of the literature debates whether autism should be viewed
as a disability, a difference, something that should be cured, or
maybe something that can be seen as an advantage in some circumstances. In reality, autism is different for each autistic person,
while there are some common characteristics. These characteristics
are cognitive in nature, are combined with hyper- and/or hypo-
sensory processing, and will affect the way in which information
is processed. The diagnostic criteria for autism within the main
diagnostic manuals are based on a medical model; terms such as
impairment and disorder are rife. It is problematic to view autism
exclusively in light of these terms, though, when it is absolutely
clear that there are individuals, clearly autistic, who do not regard
themselves in any way as disordered or impaired – or even disabled.
One term that I think valuable within this context is 'disadvantage'.
It is clear that most people with autism are at a distinct disadvantage directly as a result of being autistic within a society that does
not readily understand them.

For me, there is a huge difference between individuals being seen as disabled and being understood as being at a disadvantage; there are significant connotations to both terms, and I strongly believe that autistic adults commonly experience massive disadvantages in general day-to-day living compared to the PNT. In a sense this is fairly easy to understand – quite simply, if the majority of people think, act, communicate, process the sensory environment, etc., in a certain similar way and the autistic population differ in all these areas, then without adjustment it is highly likely that the autistic person will be disadvantaged. This is not the case for all autistic adults, but it is highly likely to be so to a greater or lesser extent for most.

The wonderful thing about this, though, is that something can be done about it! Using an extremely simplistic analogy, back in the days when being left handed was seen as 'wrong', left-handed folk were disadvantaged. They were forced to fit in with the right-handed population. As society figured out that this was non-sensical, and accepted left-handedness, the disadvantage decreased. When society then decided that it would make adjustments for its left-handed members (e.g. designing tools to be used by a left-handed person), then the 'playing field' was made more level, and the disadvantage decreased further. I firmly believe that with a paradigm shift in thinking about and understanding autism, a similar picture could unfold. I fully accept that autism with co-morbidities can be extremely disabling – but I still believe that changes in attitude, adjustments, and understanding within society can go a long way to reducing the disadvantages autistic adults frequently face. The changes do need to be considerable – but they *can* be made.

In terms of definitions of autism, it is difficult to provide a definition that isn't either so general as to be unworthy of consideration, or so unwieldy that it becomes difficult to use. Of course plenty of people have tried to define autism over the years, and there are various sets of diagnostic criteria that can be identified. The very fact that there is more than one set of diagnostic criteria establishes the fact that we don't yet have any consensus in terms of how we collectively understand autism. My way of thinking about autism (I wouldn't be so arrogant as to try and define it) is as follows:

Autism refers to a neurotype that leads to

- a cognition that is qualitatively different from that of the PNT in the way that information specific to communication, social interpretation and interaction is processed and understood;
- and to a perceptual reality of the sensory environment that differs considerably from one individual to the next.

One of the major problems when it comes to trying to define or categorize autism is that very often it is described in behavioural terms – in other words, 'people with autism do this', or 'autistic children do that'. This is simply not applicable across the whole population. If there were such a thing as 'autistic behaviour' then we would be able to identify autism simply by identifying that behaviour. There is no 'set of behaviours' that is purely autistic either – the same principle applies. There is no behaviour that an autistic person displays that isn't displayed by the non-autistic population. There is no behaviour displayed by the PNT that isn't found in the autistic population. So how can definitions be based on behaviour? I accept that there are all sorts of behaviours that are commonly associated with autism, and that some of those behaviours are seen in the majority of autistic people – but are those behaviours exclusive to autistic people? No. Are they universal to all autistic people? No. therefore, the concept of 'autistic behaviours' to my mind becomes extremely questionable.

In summary, then, my suggestion is that we understand autism as a differing neurotype that will have an *impact* on how an individual might behave – but that we can't assume that the behaviour in turn 'makes' the person autistic. Understanding autism can help massively in terms of understanding behaviour – and understanding the unique impact autism has on each individual gives us the greatest chance of understanding the autistic way of being. Understanding alone, though, may not be enough – acceptance also has a huge part to play. If we as a society were to understand and then *accept without question* the non-threatening behaviours that some autistic people need to engage in to feel comfortable, life would improve dramatically overnight. For example:

I love movement. Movement is lush; lushy delicious movement; movementy deliciousness; makes me happy, chilled, relaxed, helps me think straight; twiddly finders, spinning chairs, trampolines, bouncy castles – you name it, I love it!

But no. They look at me funny; they make me sit without swinging, talk without twiddling, work without wiggling. I am bereft. Am I causing any harm? Am I being offensive in some way? Am I causing any danger to anyone? I don't think so. Don't you understand, it's not just me being annoying? I don't just like movement, I need it; I crave it; it helps my insides settle, it helps my brain operate, it helps me make sense of the chaotic world. Why can't you let me be me . . .? Am I so very bad?

Sometimes, it isn't even understanding that is required, but only acceptance. One might not share this person's need for movement, and so maybe one cannot really understand it. But can we simply accept that it's useful, decide that it's not an issue, and allow that individual simply to be himself or herself? It's hard to see why a society *wouldn't* simply accept different, non-offensive behaviours if it makes little or no difference to the PNT and yet has a massive positive impact on autistic individuals – but autistic people will tell a different story. So many PNT lack an 'autistic theory of mind' that they find it impossible to understand the autistic perspective – but so long as they are able to *accept* the individual, the need for *understanding* is less relevant.

3

Social relationships

Life in general is supremely socially based; by this I mean that life for most people is rife with social engagements, from the minute one wakes up to the moment one goes to bed. It is critically important to clarify in this context what is meant by 'social skills'. Littered throughout the literature is the suggestion that autistic people lack social skills. This is simply not the case. I suspect very strongly that what is meant by a 'lack of social skills' actually refers to a 'lack of *PNT social skills*' – which, given that the population of autistic people is, by definition, not the PNT is hardly surprising.

Does this mean that autistic people are inherently impaired in social skills? No, absolutely not. Does it mean that autistic people are inherently impaired in PNT social skills? Probably, yes. Does this also lead to the question: are the PNT impaired in autistic social skills? The answer, unsurprisingly, is a resounding yes. I believe that autistic people can have fantastic (autistic) social skills; the number of times I have spent in the company of autistic people whose keen social skills are apparent is beyond count. The ability, for example, not to use up precious time by talking about inconsequential, trivial topics is very often seen within the autism population. Time well spent in deep reflection and observation, rather than engaging in (to the autistic individual) meaningless social chit-chat, is a skill often found in the autistic population.

This is just one example of many where it becomes apparent that 'social skills' as an all-encompassing phrase does not stand up to scrutiny. A far more effective way of understanding the social world is to understand that social skills mean something very different to the PNT compared to the autistic population. I am not suggesting that one population or the other has it 'right' – just that there is a clear, qualitative difference, and this should be respected by both parties. The concept of impairment thus becomes redundant – or, if it is to be applied, it must surely be applied to both groups.

One of my favoured ways of analogizing the concept of differ-ence rather than impairment is to apply it to my (rather wonderful) four-legged friends. To recognize that my furry, betailed quadruped Sandy Pancake Waggy Eyes (a dog) has a certain set of social skills is one thing. To then assume that the same set should apply to my equally furry betailed quadruped Pippy-Eve (the latest addition to the cat clan) would be harsh in the extreme. To admonish Pips for not wagging her tail in delight as I stroke her, or not bounding up when I come through the door would be ridiculous. Similarly, to think less of Sandy because she doesn't curl up on my knee peace-fully purring would be entirely wrong. While they share some characteristics (furriness, tails, four-leggedness), they do not share the same 'skill set'.

In the same way, while autistic and non-autistic people may share the same characteristics in some ways, they do not share the same set of social skills. And what can be seen on a daily basis with autistic children, teenagers and adults is that assumptions are made: first that autistic people *should* have the same social skill set as the PNT, and second that the same social concepts *should* be applied. This causes immense anxiety for autistic people, and gross misconceptions of autistic people from many of the PNT. Take the following case study:

> An intelligent autistic adult is going to see someone who regards him as a friend. He knocks on her door and is let in. He exclaims, 'You're looking fat and haggard today,' and follows this by giving her a hug.

This may be regarded as somewhat socially rude – inappropriate, and possibly quite offensive. The reality, at least in terms of inten-tion, is somewhat different: the friend followed this up via email, suggesting that he perhaps ought not to say such things to women. After much deliberation, the autistic adult asked whether she was upset at what he said – and if so, why? She responded by noting that she knew she was not looking her best that day, so to be told as much only affirmed it and made her feel worse.

This perplexed him – if she already knew, then why would she be upset when someone pointed it out? However, he endeavoured to explain further: 'I rarely notice how people look, because I have so few people that I care enough about to take on board such things;

so the fact that I noticed your appearance, and subsequently commented on it, is actually highly complimentary. I was worried that you were not looking so good – my comment was really my way of saying I am worried about you, and are you OK? I even made sure that I gave you a hug straight away afterwards, which surely should have made things clear!'

It can be seen from this example that intention and meaning can be easily misunderstood, or, conversely, easily understood following a translation. It is fortunate in this case that the person concerned was able to provide a translation; many autistic people are less able to do so, which makes it even more imperative that the PNT aim to understand social contexts and autistic meaning in order not to make the mistake of judging the autistic social communication within a PNT context.

Social anxiety – 'mustn't grumble'

The following account is based on the experiences of intelligent autistic folk, all of whom have spoken to me about a particular social situation (which I will refer to simply as the 'event') and how they have found it stressful. It's important to note at this point that when autistic people communicate that they are stressed, they really *are* stressed – not in a 'I'm a bit anxious' way, but often in an all-consuming manner and, very importantly, within a time frame that many of the PNT do not comprehend. Many PNT can find themselves in an anxiety-inducing situation – a job interview, a public engagement, an important exam – but what strikes me often as a qualitative difference between reports of this type of anxiety for the PNT and social anxiety reported by people with autism is the *duration* and *intensity* of the stress.

For many autistic individuals, the stress starts from the point that they are aware they have a social engagement looming; in other words, the wedding invite, or email message to meet up, or text to a party – whatever the format of the social invitation or social event – precipitates the anxiety. This can be the case even if the event itself is several weeks or months away. The stress can then last for several weeks afterwards, so one single event can cause months of increased anxiety.

For me, the anxiety and stress that perpetuates from social contact can be divided into three fairly distinct components. I will call these

- pre-event nerves
- event-itself stress
- post-event comedown.

Pre-event stress is the continuing awareness that an event is looming – and, for some, looming is an apt verb, with its connotations of being physically overwhelmed by something that is imminent. The brain can become intensely focused on going through scenario after scenario – what might happen, all the various possibilities, and all the subsequent ways in which a response could or should be proffered, what might be said, what questions should be asked, how questions should be answered, what topics of conversation are OK, what topics should be avoided, what is the appropriate thing to wear, is there an expectation to eat – if so, will it be a sit-down formal affair, and if so, who will I be sitting next to? How long do I have to be there for before leaving, who will I know, will there be physical contact involved – handshakes, hugging? Am I allowed to take my shoes off, will there be a baby crying in the venue, what toilet facilities will be available? Do I have to get 'dressed up', will I be the first to arrive, can I be the first to leave? The permutations – and therefore the rumination – are endless. The event might remain a conscious subject of thought to the point of drowning out all other rational thinking. Every waking minute holds its own level of stress. Every waking minute. Hour after hour. Day after day.

Then comes the actual event. The intense anxiety immediately before social contact is made can be neither underestimated nor overstated. To many of the PNT this cannot be easily explained – if one has never suffered from social anxiety then it must be particularly difficult to understand. Let's just say that stress levels are such that there are often very clear physical and neurological reactions akin to panic attacks. Some people report shaking, sweating, heart palpitations, even mild hallucinations prior to social contact. Even among those who do not display such characteristics, anxiety is frequently reported as being extremely high.

The event itself is often hard to describe, as many people will be so caught up in trying to work out what to say, how to under-stand the myriad of social cues, working out how, when and why responses are to be made, concentrating on not interrupting, on not being too quiet, on not saying 'the wrong thing', on trying not to stare at one spot all the time, trying to work out where one should be looking and for how long at a time, trying to under-stand the unwritten laws of physical proximity to others, trying to present as a human being totally in control of the situation when the opposite is actually the case . . . all while being bombarded by unwanted sensory stimuli that make it nigh on impossible to con-centrate on anything anyway, so that it's all a bit of a blur, and an unpleasant (that's an understatement) one at that!

Post-event comedown (aka the social hangover – thanks to Twitter #actuallyautistic posts for the phrase) can subsequently last days or weeks – and sometimes comes back to bite the victim months or years later. First is the exhaustion; the need to lie in a dark room (lit-erally or figuratively) for hours or even days. The numb brain; the emotionally drained state; the feelings of emptiness and confusion. Second, the retrospection – the rumination over what happened, why it happened, what went wrong, and what could have been done differently. Not only is this mentally shattering, it can also be a never-ending process with no clear answers. Third are the unwanted flashbacks, bringing back the negative emotional state of the event. These can occur years down the line.

So, one seemingly 'innocent' social event can cause months of pain to an autistic person.

The subtitle of this section stems from a long conversation I had with a young woman who, having made one negative remark (something along the lines of 'Do I really have to go, you know it stresses me out'), had been reprimanded by someone for grumbling about a forthcoming social event. What the young lady confided in me after the event was the number of hours her brain had been occupied in a negative way (she helpfully drew me a timeline with an associated graph of stress levels); what gave me a moment of epiphany was the fact that, taking into consideration the duration and intensity of her stress, against one relatively innocuous remark, it became clear that she is one of the least 'grumbly' people I have ever known. And yet she has a reputation for complaining about being stressed! The reality is that she is so stressed almost all the time that she very rarely, in relative terms, remarks on it.

Why do autistic people so commonly find social interaction stressful? The following are just some of the possible reasons:

- problems with social communication
- discomfort at being in the spotlight
- difficulty with group interactions.

Problems with social communication

Communication for autistic people can be problematic at the best of times, but social communication can pose particular difficulties. Being asked even supposedly simple questions can be the cause of all sorts of issues. For example, a common greeting such as 'How are you?' may elicit feelings of fear and inadequacy in the autistic person. What does this mean, she may ponder. In how much detail am I supposed to answer? Do you *really* want to know how I am, or is this simply another example of what I regard as meaningless verbal interaction – and, if so, how am I supposed to grit my teeth and lie to you? Last time I answered honestly (I was having a bad day, and I told you all about it), I got the distinct impression that I was telling you too much – but all I was doing was being honest in answering the question. And if you don't really want to know, why on earth are you asking? I know some kind of reciprocity is required here, but what is the desired response? Am I supposed to ask you in turn how you are, even though I am not in the least bit interested? I know that whatever I say, I'll spend the rest of the day worrying about it, and stressed about whether I have done the 'right' thing or not . . .

Or 'It's a lovely day, isn't it?' No, actually, it is not a lovely day. I have a terrible headache, I am dehydrated because it is so hot, the sun is making my head worse and I feel like vomiting. If you ask me, you are not only an idiot for thinking that there is a correlation between the sun shining and general loveliness, you are also highly patronizing in your belief that just because you are feeling that the day is lovely then I will be sharing in your own ideal. An honest and logical response, of course – but does it go down at all well? Most likely, no.

Or the following social exchange, with unspoken thoughts in parentheses:

DAVE (PNT)

Would you like to come to the Christmas party this year? We all notice that you haven't been since you started here nine years ago. (*I ask because I am genuinely interested in you being a part of the team and want to get to know you better.*)

ALAN (AUTISTIC ADULT)

No, thank you. (*I believe that I have responded clearly and politely.*)

DAVE (PNT)

Oh, go on, you'll love it. (*I think you need some encouragement.*)

ALAN (AUTISTIC ADULT)

Again, no, thank you. (*I am still responding politely but wondering just how it is possible that this person believes that he knows what I would love more than I do.*)

DAVE (PNT)

But you've never been before. (*I am thinking that you might like to try something new and am still being encouraging.*)

ALAN (AUTISTIC ADULT)

No, that's because I prefer not to spend time with people I don't have any relationship with other than a working one; I don't see you as a friend, or any of the team as friends for that matter, so I see little point in wasting my time with you when I have better things to do. When I am at work I want to work, when I am not at work I want to spend time with people I genuinely like, not with people whom fate/employment has happened to bring me into contact with. (*I am wondering if you need a more in-depth explanation, so I am helping you out here; I am not being in the slightest bit rude, just giving you a lovely, rational, logical account of my reasoning, despite me thinking that a 'no thank you' five minutes ago should have been the end of it. I am well aware myself that I have not been before – why do you feel the need to tell me this? I am getting irritated now.*)

DAVE (PNT)	Charming. (*I mean quite the opposite, and now believe you to be unbearably rude.*)
ALAN (AUTISTIC ADULT)	Excellent, glad that's sorted. (*I must remember to respond in that way next time, it seemed to work out well in the end.*)

The moral of the story is that if there is a lack of social under-standing (on the part of both of those involved), then the end result may not be a positive one. If the autistic person frequently gets social exchanges 'wrong' – but appears at times to get them 'right' – and yet there is no way of working out what is 'right' and what is 'wrong', then any social encounter is fraught with danger – and, therefore, potentially scary. Consider an alternative:

DAVE (PNT)	Would you like to come to the Christmas party this year? We all notice that you haven't been since you started here nine years ago. (*I ask because I am genuinely interested in you being a part of the team and want to get to know you better.*)
ALAN (AUTISTIC ADULT)	No, thank you. (*I believe that I have responded clearly and politely.*)
DAVE (PNT)	OK, no problem. If you want any more information or change your mind, let us know. (*I fully appreciate that you may not like to engage in this kind of social interaction but didn't want you to feel left out. Ever so grateful for your honesty, and I respect your decision.*)
ALAN (AUTISTIC ADULT)	Thank you for asking. Bye. (*How kind of him to ask, I may even reconsider now that I realize how pleasant he is.*)

Sadly, I find that the first scenario is more often the case than the second.

Discomfort at being in the spotlight

As a direct result of encounters like those depicted above, many autistic people simply detest being in the spotlight in social situ-ations. You will find them at the edge of parties, doing anything they can to avoid chatting. Weddings and the like can be terrifying.

Being forced to sit at tables with others where they are expected to converse can be a cause of major distress. If this is the case, obviously a good tactic is simply to avoid such situations. However, this is not always possible (or desirable), so coping mechanisms are in order. Think about giving the individual a specific task to do – some adults, for example, will happily nominate themselves as the one who will entertain the children. (This can be a massive relief all round – the autistic adult gets to play and have fun with non-judgemental kids, while the parents think he's wonderful and don't have to worry about their children!)

Interestingly, the autistic person may (sometimes, at least) be *less* stressed in more formal, structured 'under the spotlight' environments in which she plays a specific role. Acting in a play, speaking at a conference – even presenting on TV – are all examples of where an individual may be playing a clear role and is pretty much in control of the environment. However, don't make the mistake of assuming that the person's ease and confidence in that role will automatically spill over into less structured situations. Many autistic people I meet on the conference circuit will tell me that they are perfectly OK at giving the presentation, irrespective of how many people are in the audience – but the before and after can be terrifying. Seemingly, it is often the opposite for the PNT, so I am told.

Difficulty with group interactions

In a similar vein to the above, events like group work or – even more hideous for some autistic people – having to go for dinner with a partner, can induce high levels of anxiety. Consider this scenario:

> Wife tells autistic husband, 'We are going to dinner at one of my friends' houses. There'll be just eight of us altogether, we won't be more than a couple of hours. I know it's not your thing, but it's been months since we did this kind of thing together, and I'd really appreciate it. OK?'
>
> On the way home after the dinner, the wife is so pleased: 'See, that wasn't so bad. You were great – it's not that stressful after all!'

What is not apparent to the wife, through no fault of her own, is not just the anxiety her husband felt during those two hours (which was considerable), nor the intellectual and emotional strain it took to appear to 'fit in' (which was again considerable), but the heightened anxiety *from the moment he knew he had to go to the dinner* – which was approximately three weeks of constant stressful rumination over the impending event. Not only did he have to cope with those three weeks, followed by the two hours themselves – there was also all the stress afterwards as he replayed the evening over and over, trying to ensure that he had done his wife proud and hadn't let her down.

Group work – or that ubiquitous phenomenon these days, team-work – can inspire similar feelings of dread. Having to communicate in a group is tough enough, but having to do so without either saying too little or taking over by saying too much is a complication that many autistic people could do without. Knowing what to say, when to say it, how to say it, what questions to respond to, how to respond to them, who to listen to, what to do if you disagree with someone – each and every one of these individual issues can pose massive problems to an autistic person, and the combination of them can cause extreme anxiety. Similar principles can be applied in any setting – school, work, etc.

The following are the problematic aspects of social interaction that I most frequently encounter for individuals, families and, subsequently, professionals.

Peers

It is very common that society wants autistic adults to engage socially. This is entirely understandable, and is not necessarily a bad thing. It does, however, become dangerous if the autistic person is not yet ready for social engagement with unsympathetic peers. Here is an example:

Lucinda

An autistic young adult, Lucinda, is simply not engaging with others in college, and is subsequently (according to staff) not learning how to engage socially. Lucinda is, instead, doing everything she can to avoid social interaction and running away, either to hide or to engage in solitary activity at the periphery of the outdoor area. Her parent is told that she must support Lucinda and encourage her to engage with other young adults, otherwise her ability to interact socially will never improve.

Of course this is an individual case study and will not be applicable to all autistic individuals. Yet it does raise some important points that are worthy of further investigation:

- Why is Lucinda not engaging? It may well be that she does not have the necessary understanding of how to engage with others, and consequently is terrified of this kind of social engagement. It is imperative to recognize the extreme anxiety that comes with not having an intuitive understanding of how to approach others, how to respond in social situations, what the unwritten rules are, how to cope when apparent rules of the interaction are broken, etc. The point is that, unless he or she has the appropriate 'armour' in place, is it ethically and morally right to force an individual into such an environment that can cause so much genuine anxiety and/or fear?
- What is Lucinda trying to communicate through her behaviour? Is she deliberately removing herself in a highly logical manner in order to move away from a situation that causes her distress? If so, why is it that Lucinda's communication is being ignored?
- Is Lucinda happy being on her own? If so, why should she be forced into engagement she is taking herself away from?

The concept that autistic individuals will learn social engagement simply by being exposed to it is deeply flawed. As an analogy, take an English-speaking person with no classics training and give him a sheet of paper written in Latin. Make him read it – over and over again. Will he learn Latin effectively without any external input? As a parent once told me, 'If my child is forced to go out to interact with others, she has as much chance of learning social skills as she would have of learning to fly just because she keeps getting thrown out of a window!' Of course, some people love to engage with others, and get a lot out of it – but it is pertinent to be reminded that just by being exposed to social environments, the autistic person will not somehow magically develop PNT social skills.

So what are the possible solutions? First, try to ascertain why Lucinda is taking herself away from the crowd. It may be for a number of reasons, but in this case let's assume it is because of a lack of social understanding of her PNT peers. If this is the case, then she should not be forced into contact without support. Having a buddy system may be an option, but may not always work. One thing to emphasize is that it is OK for autistic people to be on their own; just because the majority of the PNT get a great deal of satisfaction from social interaction with peers, does not mean the same is true of all autistic people. Many autistic people seek isolation – not as a result of depression, but because they genuinely enjoy their own company and prefer it to that of others, and this should be perfectly acceptable.

Of course, if an individual is withdrawing for other reasons, then it may be more problematical. Having quiet areas at school or work available for unstructured social time can be a blessing for many autistic pupils who may be perfectly happy reading, or engaging in whatever stimulates them. Never underestimate the positive impact this can have – it can literally mean the difference between being able to cope at school/work, and being forced to withdraw.

Friendships

The idea that autistic people are loners and eschew social relationships, thankfully, has long since been debunked. However, it is highly probable that the nature of friendship for an autistic person may differ considerably from that of PNT friendships (although, of course, this is not always true). Frequently, autistic individuals will have a far smaller group of friends than their PNT peers – but those friendships can be far more intense and long lasting. It must be noted that it is the quality, not the quantity, of friendship that is important to the autistic population; the notion that one somehow 'ought' to have a wide group of friends can be a damaging one to the autism population. The following examples depict very different social beings, each of them an autistic individual:

Mark is commonly found in his room, isolated, never showing any signs of wanting to go out. He doesn't appear to have any friends, and he refuses any invitation to socialize with his work colleagues. In Mark's case, although he is not particularly traditional in his social needs, it is apparent that he is perfectly happy with his own company and prefers it to anyone else's. This is perfectly OK, and yet so often people are judged to somehow be 'lacking' when they exist in a similar way to Mark.

Anna also spends a lot of time in her room. Very differently from Mark, however, Anna is miserable, and frequently complains that she is lonely and wants friends, but simply can't seem to get anyone to like her. In this case some kind of support clearly needs to be put in place. Many autistic adults are isolated not out of choice but out of fear, anxiety and stress – and yet they crave time with others.

Leo is trying hard to make friends, but frequently gets rejected from 'the group'. He keeps going back to the same group, and meets the same fate over and over again, which causes him to wonder what on earth is going on. He is confused and hurt by the way he is being treated. This is by no means an uncommon situation – and it is essential here to note that very often autistic adults may not 'learn from their mistakes' in the same way as the PNT might (which may have some good logic behind it – see the section on trust, p. 45). Leo is an example of someone who may well benefit from specific skills training, both to help him understand and develop his own PNT social skills, and also to learn more about how and why the PNT behave in the way they do.

Duncan does have a circle of friends. They are very understanding in the main, but as he gets older his friends are growing increasingly irritated by the fact that Duncan seems to be best friends one minute and appears to turn his back on them the next – and then wants to be best friends again when it suits him. Many autistic people simply assume that their friends know the same things they know themselves. Duncan means no harm – and, therefore, his friends 'should' know this and therefore not be offended. The reality is that Duncan can only cope with friends for certain periods of time, and then needs to recharge his 'social batteries' before exposing himself to the people game once again.

Jen appears to be desperate to make friends and tries everything she can to 'fit in'. On occasion she has even been known to play pranks on others to try and get people to like her, to the point that she has been accused of bullying. Jen is another person who wants friends, but in her case simply does not understand that the way to make friends may differ from her perception of how to go about it.

What the above examples demonstrate is that autistic adults – just like the PNT – will have different levels of sociability, which means that each person needs to have his or her preferences understood; if support was specific to presentation alone, it would very likely that the autistic adult would end up with pressure to engage when he didn't want (or need) to.

Development of skills

It is undeniable that society has reasonable expectations that most people, those with autism included, will exhibit a certain level of social skills. Being polite, recognizing the impact of one's behaviour on those around, listening to others – these are examples of skills that may well be useful for an autistic person to first recognize, and then learn, should the need arise (i.e. if they don't already have such skills). I think that learning such aspects of social interaction is best done from as early an age as possible, and incorporated as a routine, rather than being expected at an intuitive level. If a verbal and/or mental routine is established early on in life, then it is far easier for the autistic person to successfully engage with those around her than if she has to learn an intangible 'skill' later on. For example, being taught to 'be polite' may be extremely difficult for an autistic individual – after all, this can have many different connotations, each applicable in differing contexts. On the other hand, being taught a *routine* whereby the expectation is to respond to social questions (and being explicitly taught what may be useful as responses) might be far more 'autism friendly' and beneficial in the long run. In the same way that a morning routine, or a toileting routine, can be taught so that it becomes automatic, so can a certain level of social routines.

I do not believe that an autistic person will 'grow into' a PNT social mindset with age; this is not how autistic people learn or develop. Certainly, as one ages, one's ability to socially interact may change considerably – as will one's social needs. As a child an individual may not have any interest in friends, but as the child grows older this may change to a burning desire for friendship.

Teaching skills can be done in foresight, and in hindsight. I particularly like developing knowledge and understanding using games (in order to develop foresight). For example, if an individual is particularly interested in a computer game, the characters in the game can be used to examine what social interaction is taking place, what the benefits are of engaging socially, and how a particular character might do things better – as well as noting the positive aspects when they do something socially 'well'. Using foresight can also help develop understanding of cause and effect, something that in a social context can be very difficult to grasp. Teaching a conscious process of thinking about social behaviour can be massively beneficial.

Hindsight can be used to discuss a situation that has perhaps ended poorly for whatever reason. Exploring the process and identifying critical aspects of how one might have behaved differently, and recognizing the implications of this in terms of differing outcomes, can work very well. Much has been written about this concept using resources like Social Stories™ (for more information, see <www.carolgraysocialstories.com>), so I won't repeat what others are better at writing!

4

Echopraxic behaviour: 'masking' and being a good actor

A major problem for autistic people, one that can occur either at school and later in life at work or in social situations, stems from a specific skill that many people with autism appear to possess and use as a coping mechanism. Many individuals are able to mimic others' behaviour, and do so to enable them to exist (or cope) in a PNT-dominated environment with a reduced chance of 'standing out'. I suspect that the reason behind what is called echopraxic* behaviour (i.e. the copying of other people's actions) is actually very similar to the motive for forms of behaviour sometimes observed in the rest of the population. Most people do not like to be the 'odd one out' – and one way of standing out is by not conforming behaviourally in a social situation.

As a result of similar cognitive and learning styles, the PNT tend to find it relatively easy to conform and understand intuitively how they should behave in most situations. However, there are – infrequently – times when it is less clear how one should behave. In such situations it is common for the person (consciously or subconsciously) to watch what those around him are doing and then follow suit. A good example of this is the person who does not usually attend church but finds himself at a service, for whatever reason. It is relatively easy for that person to copy those around him, standing up, kneeling, singing, etc., when they do – this is classic echopraxic behaviour at its most obvious. Of course, there are examples of this in more subtle forms throughout life; indeed, child development is rife with echopraxia, as children mimic those around them as a way of learning how to behave. The drive to

---

* I use echopraxia in this chapter to mean deliberate and/or involuntary copying of behaviour – in more clinical arenas a different definition may apply.

conform and the desire not to stand out means that such echopraxic behaviour is a beneficial learning tool for the PNT child
– but the subconscious learning process possessed by the individual
means that as life goes on, the exigency for copying behaviour
diminishes until it is almost entirely obsolete.

However, this is often not the case for the autistic person. Autistic
individuals often lack the indirect learning process that supports
the subconscious development of such skills, so as time ticks on the
individual is left further and further behind in terms of the innate
ability to understand behaviour in social circumstances. While the
PNT become more and more adept at 'fitting in' as time passes, so
the autistic individual can stand out more and more. Many individuals find this extremely distressing, and will seek ways to avoid
it if at all possible – and one seemingly excellent way of coping in
such difficult circumstances is to hone masking skills to such an
extent that their behaviour replicates that of people around them
so that, in effect, they appear to 'fit in' in the same way as the PNT
peer group. While this may seem wholly appropriate and positive –
and, indeed, it can be a very useful coping mechanism – it must also
be viewed with caution. The following are some of the potential
pitfalls for the autistic person engaging in echopraxic behaviour:

- the masking of very real skill issues; giving the impression of
  ability, resulting in a lack of appropriate support and recognition;
- exhaustion;
- lack of understanding of oneself;
- intense stress when trying to understand what is the 'right'
  behaviour;
- a build-up of stress leading to meltdown.

The masking of skill issues

It is hugely ironic that having great skill in one area can actually be so
problematic in another – and yet this is often the case for the autistic
adult who has good masking skills. In a sense there can be a direct
correlation between the individual's masking ability and the lack of
understanding on the part of those around that person in terms of
his or her support needs. In fact, there is a strong argument that if
an individual *requires* masking skills then he also requires recogni-

tion that he is finding social situations problematic, and thus needs understanding, and possibly support. However, the individual with honed copying skills may also be the person who is least likely to be observed as needing additional understanding and support. This can be a major problem at school or at work, where pupils or employees mask their very real needs by copying others, and are so accomplished at doing so that their actual support needs go unrecognized.

It is common in such circumstances for any pleas for support to be met with responses ranging from bewilderment to outright scorn. Employers, colleagues, acquaintances, friends – even family members – may be so used to seeing what they believe to be a person who shows no signs of struggling that they find it impossible to accept that the reality may be vastly different. The result is that often others refuse to accept that the individual is struggling and requires very specific input, and the individual remains unsupported. This can be a very dangerous situation for the autistic person to be in, and every effort should be made to modify the misplaced impression of the school, employer, partner or friend.

Judging from the accounts to be found in blogs and the like, it appears that acting skills are more prevalent in the female autistic population – which may account for some of the difficulties that women have in getting their autism recognized. Many individuals identify what a huge gap there is between the way the person presents (i.e. his or her observable behaviour) and the reality of what's going on at a neurological level. The disparity can be huge – the calm, 'appropriate' exterior 'face' often belies the extreme chaos and frantic brain activity that is unseen. While on the one hand this allows the person to 'get by' in social situations, at work and so on, it can subsequently be impossible for him or her to persuade anyone that an enormous amount of effort actually goes into acting in this particular way.

There is a possible solution. All people need time to 'be themselves'; the more society accepts an autistic way of being, the less likely it is that autistic people will have to 'hide' behind a façade that society deems to be 'appropriate'. This is, of course, a long-term solution, as it will take considerable time for society to understand and accept autistic presentations (i.e. ways of behaving), however logical and meaningful to the autistic individual. In the meantime, providing 'safe' environments in which individuals can relax and recharge – i.e. be themselves – could be of great benefit.

Similarly, having within a work context people who genuinely understand the autistic presentation to engage with, for example, can go a long way towards reducing stress. Having people to talk to whereby the individual is not having to constantly explain herself may be rare, but it can also make a critical difference between well-being on the one hand and major distress on the other. In addition, society as a whole needs to be far more ready to accept what autistic people are saying – if autistic people can only ever 'be themselves' when isolated from the rest of the community, then their voice must be heard and accepted; far too often when autistic adults explain what their reality is really like, they are dismissed, simply because some people refuse to acknowledge that if they can't see it for themselves, then it can't be true. Actually listening to autistic adults and accepting their reality will go a long way towards reducing problems.

Exhaustion

Having to consciously copy other people can be extremely tiring for the individual, and levels of energy can be tested to the extreme. Often, the individual spends much of her energy throughout the day just making sure she fits in, to the extent that at the end of the working day her energy levels are exhausted, and thus her ability to continue coping in any way can be minimal. It is common in these circumstances for the individual's presentation (or behaviour) at home to be in stark contrast to her presentation during the day; in a similar vein to the point made above, it is often extremely difficult to persuade 'externals' (i.e. people at work who are not on hand to observe changes in presentation at home) that this is the case. Again, this means that the necessary support and understanding are often not forthcoming. The mental energy that is required to constantly wear a mask cannot be underestimated, nor can the impact the effort will subsequently have on the individual, both from day to day and in the longer term.

Lack of understanding of oneself

If an individual habitually copies others, then the long-term repercussions can be detrimental indeed. The longer people are forced into behaving in a manner that is not a true reflection of who they are, the greater the chance that they will begin to lose their sense of self, their own identity, and their understanding of who they actually are. This is clearly a potential problem of considerable proportions, and it is one that is eminently evident in many adults with autism who have had to alter their behaviour to better suit those around them. Everyone needs time to 'be themselves' – and this is just as true for autistic adults as it is for anyone else. The problem is that because there is often a huge disparity between the masked presentation and true presentation of self for the autistic adult, there are fewer opportunities in which to relax and recuperate.

Intense stress as to 'right' behaviour

Quite aside from the intellectual energy needed to adequately copy others, there can be extra emotional pressure for individuals who lack the ability to know whether or not their behaviour is acceptable. Many autistic people will try to alter their behaviour in order to attempt to blend in, but do not know at any point whether or not they will be successful. Ruminating and agonizing over each social contact can be intensely distressing, and in the longer term can easily lead to mental health problems.

Imagine what life would be like if one had no idea whether what one says to another person would be either accepted, ridiculed or taken as offensive, when one was desperately trying to do 'the right thing'. In addition one would have the added stress of noting that no one else seemed to have any problems at all in doing 'the right thing'. It is not difficult to realize the immense pressure this puts on the autistic person, nor to realize that if no action is taken the individual is in an extremely vulnerable position.

Build-up of stress leading to meltdown

As a result of the factors above, or any permutation of them, the individual may experience such a build-up of stress throughout the day that there will be an eventual and inevitable release in the form of a meltdown (i.e. an involuntary release of emotion which can take several different forms, and can be deeply unsettling or even traumatic for the individual). Each person will display this in his or her own way, but rarely, if ever, is such a state to be welcomed. Often the meltdown will be detrimental to all involved, not least the individual herself. It is not uncommon for the individual to be left feeling guilty, ashamed, and negative about herself – and all she was trying to do is fit in. Rarely are such meltdowns evident in the environment that is causing the stress, however – it is far more common for them to occur in a 'safe' place, often at home.

Echopraxia can be a wonderful coping mechanism, allowing the individual to 'get away' with not having the intuitive skills of the PNT interaction. However, it can be a problematic way of coping. While patterns will invariably differ from person to person, a theme that occurs with worrying frequency can be seen within the autistic population. Here is an example of this common scenario:

1 The individual is in a situation disturbing to her, for example at work, and she does not intuitively know how to respond.
2 She consciously makes the effort to fit in by using her echopraxic skills.
3 Those around her have no idea that she is making this effort – all they see is the external behaviour which appears to them to be similar to everyone else's, albeit with some discrepancies.
4 As a result, the employer has no idea that the individual is struggling on a day-to-day basis, and she is left to her own devices.
5 The individual is either forced to cope with extreme levels of daily stress, or she has a breakdown.

This may appear to be a rather dramatic view of the process – but it isn't. Such scenarios are all too common, and it is easy to understand why. It is crucial to overcome these issues to ensure that the autistic person is not left in such a vulnerable position, and that she or he receives appropriate support.

Here, the age-old problem resurfaces. How can other people be persuaded that what they believe to be true is not necessarily an accurate representation of what is occurring for the autistic individual? Hopefully, as autism is better understood, people will accept that the appearance of 'getting along fine' can be profoundly misleading. Listening to those who know better – parents, partners, friends and, above all, the autistic individual – will hopefully become the norm rather than the exception.

Once the issue has been established, the next logical question is, what can be done about it? Ideally, the environment would be adapted so that the individual did not need to force himself to behave unnaturally – in other words, he could behave as a perfectly happy autistic person without fear of compromise. Sadly, this is rarely possible – but we can live in hope. An alternative is that circumstances can be adjusted to better suit the person – the making of changes in employment environments is a good example of this. Not forcing the individual to engage in activities that cause excessive distress will certainly help to alleviate some issues; for example, if an individual finds unstructured face-to-face meetings highly distressing, get rid of them (the meetings, that is, not the employee)! Similarly, if much of the stress at work relates to those horrible social activities, the unstructured times of supposed fun – staff breaks, or social activity outside work – expectations should not be placed on any staff member to join in. *There should be no pressure whatsoever for autistic employees to engage in any activity that is not within their job description.*

The most important message, I believe, in relation to masking is to listen to *and believe* autistic adults when they are able to articulate their realities. When someone tells us how exhausting life can be, let's not force them to somehow prove it, but instead let's accept that this is the case. Autistic adults may well have spent their whole lives trying to get across what life is like for them, and having someone actually listen and accept what they say can be a lifesaver.

5

Anxiety

Most autistic adults suffer – and I do mean suffer – from higher levels of anxiety than non-autistic adults (this is on average – of course being autistic does not automatically mean one is anxious, nor does the autistic population hold a monopoly on being stressed). Stress and anxiety can be caused by many different factors, but I have chosen here just some that are important to acknowledge.

One premise runs throughout this chapter – being autistic does *not* mean that one will automatically be anxious or have raised stress levels (remember the magic equation – autism + environment = outcome). Therefore, anxiety *can* be alleviated – even if not necessarily with ease. Anxiety in adults is often so ingrained that you may feel life will never be any different; and, sometimes, issues are so deeply rooted that any reduction in anxiety may be a hugely demanding task. Very often the changes in life that need to be made require substantial adjustment – not in you, but in the people and/or in the environment surrounding you that are making life so difficult. It's hard enough trying to live your own life without trying to influence the behaviour of people around you! However, recognizing what can cause anxiety for autistic adults and making appropriate adjustments can make a huge difference to the individual.

In reference to the terms 'stress' and 'anxiety', it's worth noting that these are conscious states. The individual *knows* that she is stressed. Many PNT go through long periods of life without waking up to find that their first thought is 'I am stressed, I can feel it' – and yet many autistic adults experience this every single day. Reducing anxiety, therefore, is an extremely important goal. The following are some of the reasons that underlie heightened anxiety.

Pressure

A common reaction to pressure for all of us, to one degree or another, is increased stress and heightened anxiety, which can in some cases lead to panic. While not all autistic people will demonstrate the kind of behaviour associated with pressurized situations, many will; this is not a result simply of 'being autistic', but a result of being autistic in an environment that frequently applies pressure far more to the autistic individual than it does to the 'average' member of the PNT. It is interesting to note that while the PNT population tend to become anxious over what may be regarded as 'major events', it is not uncommon for autistic people to become anxious over seemingly less problematic situations. Be very wary of making such an assumption, though – to the autistic person what she faces may induce unbearable anxiety, to the point of meltdown or shutdown.

To clarify those terms, *meltdown* denotes behaviours that appear to the ignorant outsider to be utterly out of context as a reaction to the situation, and may be destructive (to oneself or others or the environment) and in many cases quite frightening; *shutdown* is a passive reaction – sleeping or 'freezing' – where the individual literally appears to 'shut down' for a while. The latter may appear less problematic; the reality is that this is not always the case. There is an argument that the passive reaction, the shutdown, does not balance out the stress, but simply defers it, while the meltdown provides a cathartic release. Either way, it is clear that the individual will be damaged by every exposure to a situation that causes such heightened anxiety that the only course of reaction is meltdown or shutdown.

Pressure can be found in all sorts of situations – but one of the most common themes is that many problematic environments include other people. There is so much pressure with respect to the need for immediate verbal reciprocity, for example, and this in many cases can be relatively simply avoided. It's always worth thinking about whether verbal communication – as opposed to communication via email or text, for example – is necessary. Other examples of pressure include any situation in which the autistic person is placed in the spotlight (many will spend huge levels of energy trying to avoid this), being forced into social situations, or being in an environment in which the 'rules of engagement' are unclear.

Verbal communication and trust

It may seem odd to suggest that verbal communication is a direct cause of anxiety, but for the autistic adult this can certainly be the case. As noted in Chapters 2 and 3, there is much within PNT communication that is stressful – but over and above that are the degrees of ambiguity and downright inaccuracies of verbal interplay that can cause so much distress to the individual. The following scenarios illustrate some aspects of this issue:

Sam wakes up one morning, and as always she immediately checks her diary to remind herself of what she has planned for the day. She sees that she is due to meet her friend, Vicki, for lunch at 12.30 p.m. in a café she has never been to. Already, she's feeling on edge. She adores Vicki but she's never been to this café, so she feels a looming sense of dread of the unknown. Still, it's something she needs to get over as otherwise she won't get to see her best friend. As always, Sam is meticulous with her timekeeping and is ready ahead of schedule. She's checked (and double-checked) the bus times and has ensured that she'll be in plenty of time. She waits outside the café, nervous of the impending social encounter and the unknown café. But wait . . . where is Vicki? She checks her watch: 12.31 p.m. Then she checks her phone: yes, it's 12.31 p.m. – and no messages from Vicki.

Five minutes later, Vicki arrives, with a mutual friend, Lianne. 'Hi Sam, bumped into Lianne so I asked her if she'd like to join us. How're you doing?'

Sam's internal dialogue goes as follows: 'I'm crushed. You said quite clearly we would meet at 12.30 p.m. and it's 12.36 . . . Where have you been . . . you said 12.30 p.m., I know you did. You lied . . . why is Lianne here? . . . I'm not prepared for this . . . you said 12.30 p.m. . . . oh no . . . 12.30 p.m. . . . it's 12.36 p.m. . . . lied to again . . . you never said anything about inviting Lianne . . . why did you lie . . . why isn't it just you and me as I expected . . . you must hate me to do this to me . . . 12.30 p.m. . . . 12.36 p.m. . . . I can't speak . . . I'm crushed, devastated . . . I don't understand any of this . . . I need to get out of here . . .'

Sam runs away.

Joe is in a team meeting at work, something that always causes him stress but which he knows he is expected to attend. As always, as his levels of anxiety rise, Joe's reliance on clear communication increases.

Joe's boss, Pete, states: 'Right, these meetings are going to be held more regularly from now on.'

Joe: 'I don't understand, we hold the team meetings every Friday at 10 a.m.'

Pete: 'Yes, thanks for that, Joe – but I'm saying we need to hold them more regularly, so . . .'

Joe (interrupting): 'But we can't be any more regular than we currently are. They are every Friday at 10 a.m. . . . ?'

Pete: 'Yes, but as I was about to say, we will now have an additional meeting on a Tuesday.'

Joe: 'So they will be just as regular then . . .'

Pete: 'Joe, what are you talking about?'

Joe: 'It's OK, it's a common mistake. You aren't in fact referring to regularity, you're talking about frequency. What you should have said is we are going to meet more frequently. Don't worry, lots of people get it wrong . . .'

Later that day Joe is called into his line manager's office to explain why he showed his boss such a level of disrespect in front of the whole team over such a petty detail.

It is often the case that the level of linguistic accuracy displayed by an autistic adult, combined with the PNT's linguistic inaccuracy, causes a misunderstanding – and, usually, the autistic individual is subsequently deemed to be the one at fault. In reality the mistake has been made by the PNT, and yet it's the autistic individual who ends up with the disadvantage. In terms of the implications of this for anxiety, consider the following:

> Tanya *knows* that some of what her colleague states turns out to be true;
>
> Tanya *knows* that some of what her colleague states turns out to be false.

How is Tanya supposed to know whether or not to believe anything her colleague states?

This can then lead to huge issues of trust – being lied to (however insignificant what is said might seem to the PNT) can be a cruel blow to the autistic adult who has likely had a lifetime of being let down to contend with anyway. To many such people, *any* communication breakdown, however trivial it might seem, can lead to a loss of trust. 'Vicki was only five minutes late' might be an immediate PNT reaction, in that surely it doesn't really matter. Mark was simply using one word incorrectly, 'and surely that's just being pedantic'. And yet the autistic person's reaction is far more likely to be one of being let down, lied to, traumatized, chastised simply for being correct, made to feel terrible just because of her need to know the 'truth', being made to feel inadequate because no one else has an issue with these things. All in all, the negative impact cannot be underestimated. Is it any wonder, then, that the individual feels less and less secure in terms of trusting others? Or that you always have some level of anxiety because you never quite know who is trustworthy?

Another aspect of communication that can cause anxiety is the bewildering nature of what people say to the autistic person. Many autistic adults use language within their own, logical parameters. But most of the PNT use language in quite different ways, and think nothing of using language to engage with one another in a manner that is rarely, if ever, questioned. Truisms, redundancies, pleonasms, tautology – from a strictly autistic logical perspective these can be extremely difficult to digest. Here are some statements followed by the autistic thought process in response:

'She loves him so much, he's the love of her life, she's never loved anyone quite like it . . .' (*OK, I get it, the first five words were sufficient.*)

'So she showed me her engagement ring, a beautiful round platinum one.' (*Yes, all rings are round, don't you know . . .*)

'She gave birth last night to a lovely little baby girl' (*Are you serious? A* little *baby – who would have thought!*)

'And she followed it up by giving birth to another, she's the proud mummy to two twins!'(Two *twins – as opposed to how many?*)

The list could go on – and on. But suffice to note that autistic language and PNT language can (and, perhaps, should) be seen as different things. Many autistic adults report that before they respond they have to consciously translate what they have heard to make sure they have understood it (which is not always an accurate process), and then formulate a response, doing their best to ensure that the response will not be taken 'the wrong way'. By this time the response may be outdated, or the person will think you're simply ignoring them, or that you are just plain rude!

Stability and resistance to change

Many individuals have a so-called 'autistic resistance to change'. This can create major problems when it comes to issues of transition, be it the physical transition from one environment to another or the major life changes that occur as a child grows into adulthood. Transition by definition will involve change. Only by addressing the issue of change, and the problems associated with it, can individuals be supported appropriately. Not only might the individual display anxiety over impending major changes, he may also display extreme stress over what might appear to the PNT eye as minor or trivial changes in everyday life.

So often, the PNT reaction is to assume that the change is unimportant, thus judging the autistic person via a PNT perspective – which then often leads to a potentially damaging and stressful lack of acknowledgement of just how important 'sameness' is to the autistic individual. In some cases it may even be that the individual is almost forced to 'put up' with change simply because the PNT considers change to be immaterial and refuses to recognize just how stressful it can be for the individual. I believe that, actually, many autistic people are not in the slightest bit bothered by a lot of changes – but they do have an extreme interest in keeping certain aspects of life the same. This is different from saying that 'autistic individuals are resistant to all change' – which is not accurate at all. What is perhaps more valid is the notion of individual *autistic* resistance to change – i.e. an individual may have an understandable resistance to certain things changing that are of significant importance to that individual.

One of the defining manifestations of the way in which individuals are affected by autism is the degree to which change, in various guises, can cause distress. Of course, individuals will be affected in different ways dependent on a plethora of factors, but it is fair to say that the vast majority, if not all, individuals with autism will experience an inherent resistance to change in one form or another during part or all their lives. The key question is why? What is it about sameness that is so important to the individual, and what – if anything – can be done about it?

The very nature of 'change' needs to be explored when discussing the 'autistic resistance to change', lest PNT assumption be placed on the individual, leading to a lack of true understanding of the difficulties faced by that individual. I would argue that autistic individuals process information in a considerably different way from the PNT, and that it is dangerous to ever make assumptions concerning an individual, irrespective of how he or she presents. 'Change', then, in the way which may typically be understood may be very different from the concept of 'change' which causes problems for the autistic individual. The hypothesis outlined below explores one possible reason why, from the perspective of the autistic person, individuals find 'change' problematic. Please note that, in relation to autism, when I refer to 'change' I am talking in the main about unexpected change; planned changes tend to be less stressful (though they may cause problems as well).

It is important to note that this hypothesis does not explain the entire concept of 'resistance to change', nor will it be valid for every individual. It has been introduced simply to support the point that we must endeavour, at all times, to understand the autism-specific perspective, and not fall into the trap of making PNT assumptions.

Resistance to change: a hypothesis

This hypothesis is based on the principle that everyone needs a great deal of stability in their day-to-day living to feel secure. Stability is 'created' in a number of ways but, fundamentally, is based on aspects of life such as:

- shared communication and social understanding
- understanding other people, e.g. their behaviour
- emotional recognition of others
- a shared sensory environment
- predictability
- fulfilled expectations.

Most PNT enjoy, to a significant degree, all the above. Communication between individuals is not often greatly problematic. Most of the time people understand why those around them behave the way they do. Emotional recognition and understanding does not cause problems, the sensory environment is likely to be interpreted in the same (or a similar) way to the next person, and daily life is predictable and expectations are fulfilled. If one were to argue, as I would, that these key areas are what creates an overall sense of stability, then it may be argued that the PNT population tend to lead essentially fairly stable lives. Naturally there are exceptions to the rule, but for most PNTs, for most of the time, life is highly stable.

The hypothesis, it then follows, argues that for the same reasons that life is stable for the PNT, it is potentially very unstable for the autistic individual. It is highly likely that for each key area which offers stability for the PNT, the opposite will be true for those with autism. The autistic individual will have core differences which decrease stability for him in the PNT environment in a directly opposite way to that which creates stability for the PNT in that same environment. Thus, for example, a different understanding of social interaction decreases stability in a world where social interaction plays an important part of everyday life. The interpretation of verbal and non-verbal communication alike greatly disadvantages the autistic individual in an environment in which communication plays an enormous part.

I would argue that autistic individuals attempt to create stability for themselves (though not necessarily consciously), and that this can be manifested in an infinite number of ways. The individual develops 'acute' reliability on her idiosyncratic areas of stability. When these areas of 'acute' stability are changed, the individual is likely to become greatly distressed.

For example, extreme reactions to what is seemingly innocuous change can often be observed in the autistic individual. It appears that the 'little things' can be of great importance to such an individual. It may be difficult for the PNT to accept that a minor change in a routine can be hugely problematic in the world of autism unless understood from the perspective of the individual. In essence, what is happening can be laid out in a simple formula that can be applied to anyone, autistic or not:

increased stability ➔ reduced stress/anxiety ➔ a happier person

The major difference between the PNT and the autistic person in many cases is that global stability is not based on the same areas of life. As noted, for the PNT, global stability comes from the various aspects of life that include communication, social understanding, and so on. If autistic individuals cannot rely on these aspects of life for their stability, where do they get it from? I believe that many such individuals rely on aspects of life either that are totally within their control, or on aspects that appear to remain the same. Such criteria are rarely fulfilled – for many autistic people, few areas of life are totally in their control, and not many aspects of life are reliably constant. Routines can be an area of huge comfort and stability, as they are often in the control of the individual. When control is taken away from the individual, or the routine is broken, major distress sets in. If the individual has to place a huge amount of reliance on these areas to allow himself global stability, then it is easy to understand the distress caused when those areas are changed – this is the 'autistic resistance to change'.

Take, for example, a morning routine. The individual regularly has a set routine, including having her breakfast with the same cereal and the same amount of milk, in the same white bowl with a red rim around it. One morning the bowl is replaced by a white one of the same size and shape, but with a blue rim. The individual reacts by throwing the bowl across the room. This may appear to be aggressive, unreasonable behaviour. However, I would argue that it is a perfectly understandable reaction if the individual relies so heavily on her routine, and the detail of the routine, to provide stability for her day. It is common for individuals to pay particular attention to detail, rather than to 'the wider picture'. This strengthens the understanding that change for the individual may not be similar in nature to the more global changes that the PNT find difficult.

To look at it from another perspective, if a 12-hour period were to be broken down into time during which the individual is stable and time during which she is unstable, following the hypothesis it would be argued that the PNT will experience stability for a high percentage of that time. The converse may be true for the autistic individual. Reducing 'stability' by, for example, 5 per cent may have little effect on the PNT, who has a great deal of stability over and above that. For an autistic person, who may only have 5 per cent of her entire day that she can 'rely' on – any change in those areas of stability will lead to major distress and anxiety.

The hypothesis concludes that change is most distressing to the individual when that change occurs in the areas of life that are relied upon to create stability. Thus, if an individual relies on always walking the same route to work, for example, and it creates stability for him, then a change in the route to work may cause major anxiety.

In order to alleviate the distress caused by change, support should be offered to the person around those key elements in life which he or she finds problematic. Thus, by using appropriate communication systems, developing an awareness of other people's behaviour, emotional recognition, etc. the general level of stability (what I refer to as 'global stability') of the person with autism should increase. Prior to supportive intervention the individual may have large periods of instability from day to day. If that instability can be reduced, then ultimately, it should decrease the level of the person's reliance on the areas of stability he or she has 'created'. In effect, the more stability an individual enjoys, the less problematic any changes in his or her areas of 'enforced stability' become.

Other causes of anxiety

Here are some further examples of what might lead people with autism to experience intense difficulty:

- working to deadlines
- responding to questions
- making choices.

All these can be linked to resistance to change and the notion of global stability, but there are some subtle differences. A simple but effective way of thinking about why an autistic individual might respond so differently from the PNT to, for example, a verbal question, is to establish a mental equation firmly in your mind:

The greater the overall stress = the greater the inability of the individual to cope with day-to-day life.

While this is a simple equation on paper, it is far more complex in reality, as the individual himself may be unaware of the stresses he is under, and they can be difficult to discern. In a sense, one should take the lead from the individual – if he is clearly struggling, for example, to work to a deadline (i.e. the response is meltdown or shutdown), then a reasonable assumption would be that stresses (known or unknown) are too high to enable the individual to respond effectively.

Of course there are plentiful other reasons why an individual might struggle with the things noted above; lack of global stability is not the only one. However, it is worth bearing in mind that issues around these areas are often an indication of low stability and high levels of stress, and should be taken seriously.

Working to deadlines

While many autistic people love the idea of deadlines and crave the clarity they provide, others simply cannot cope with the pressure they impose. This is extraordinarily problematic in almost all educational fields, as well as in employment – but it does not mean that the individual cannot meet the requirements of her course, job, etc. Interestingly, reducing the pressure to work to a deadline alleviates the pressure *for some people*, allowing the individual to engage at her own pace and subsequently meet the original requirements.

Responding to questions

It may be that, on occasion, when asked a question the mind of the autistic person either goes into overdrive, or quietly but firmly shuts down. The former reaction can be debilitating and stressful for the individual, the latter can be hugely irritating for the person who has asked the question. Either way, *the autistic person is not at fault*. It is not a deliberate wind-up, nor a means to annoy or frustrate. It may be simply an unavoidable neurological reaction that indicates deeper levels of stress. In such cases the worst thing to do would be to insist on an answer. Far better to leave it for another time, or leave it altogether if possible. Alternatively, non-face to face questions (e.g. email) tend to be far less problematic and are to be encouraged.

Making choices

There are certain choices that some individuals find impossible to cope with – open-ended choices are often of a type that cause huge problems to the autistic person (by definition, an open-ended question can have an unlimited number of answers; logically it is impossible to select between an infinite number of choices). It may be difficult for the PNT to appreciate this, as often such choices are easy to make for them; this is a classic case of judging the autistic person from a PNT perspective, and should be avoided at all costs. For people who find making choices difficult, either allow them the time needed, come back at a later date, or break the choice down to a much simpler level. Generally, giving options from which to choose is far easier for the autistic individual to deal with than offering an open-ended choice.

To conclude, anxiety and autism are very often extremely unwelcome bedfellows. There is not, however, a direct equation between autism and elevated anxiety. If we accept that it's autism *plus the environment* that causes the anxiety, and we acknowledge that one cannot stop a person being autistic, then logic dictates that if we want that person's anxiety to diminish, then we must change the environment.

6

Sensory profile

Included in some diagnostic criteria is a growing recognition that autistic individuals process their sensory environment in ways that differ from the PNT experience. It is extremely important to recognize this, for very often the sensory environment can have a dramatic impact on such individuals; this can be a positive thing, but it can also be negative. It is crucial, therefore, that all autistic individuals have a clear understanding of their own sensory profile in order to understand what environment is best suited to them. A clear sensory profile will also help others to gain a better understanding of your needs, including within the workplace. I have deliberately addressed this chapter to 'you', meaning any autistic reader.

Your sensory profile can change over time; indeed, it might change literally from one moment to the next! Being able to recognize when and how the sensory environment is affecting you can help enormously in daily living. In brief, you may be either hyper-sensitive, or hypo-sensitive, or both, in any or all of your sensory domains. In plain language this means that compared to a usual sensory experience you might be highly sensitive, or less sensitive than the PNT, in any or all the ways in which you process (i.e. experience) touch, sights, sounds, smells and tastes. In addition you may have some differences in the system that governs your proprioception (awareness of one's body) and your vestibular system (which deals with balance and co-ordination).

This chapter identifies some areas of sensory processing that might affect you. Of course, it goes without saying (I hope) that one person's sensory nightmare might be another's sensory heaven – such is the nature of autism! The following list is by no means exhaustive, but will give you (and those around you) some idea of how the sensory environment could influence you, with some suggestions as to how one might try and reduce any negative effects.

As stated, your sensory experiences might change over time – but it's worth noting that they can also be influenced by factors such as physical well-being, emotional stability and levels of anxiety. In other words, it is far more likely that you will undergo negative sensory experiences if you are feeling anxious, for example, than when you are in good overall health.

One final point. Sometimes it's incredibly difficult to get other people to accept that your own sensory experiences are real to you. Don't fall into the trap of thinking that, just because they don't find the noise of a baby crying physically painful, it isn't a very real issue for you!

Your sensory profile – some things you may want to consider

Touch

Do you show sensory sensitivity with touch? For example, how do you react to the following?

- *Fabric*. Do you show a preference for/dislike of specific types? For some, the touch of certain materials can be offensive to the point of huge discomfort, or even pain. It's well worth recognizing this and experimenting so that you are as comfortable as possible. It can be a massive disadvantage to be constantly aware of what you are wearing because it's not comfortable. Sometimes just the slightest change can make all the difference – not doing the top button up on a shirt, or wearing a tight-fitting T-shirt underneath, may make the difference between being able to tolerate clothing and not.
- *Sleeves*. Do you need to have either short sleeves or long sleeves? Some people simply crave one or the other!
- Do you find *labels in clothes* uncomfortable? This can be a huge one – many individuals find the sensation of labels in clothes simply unbearable, and cutting them out or unstitching them is the only option.
- Do you mind *seams in socks*? Similarly to labels, the seams of socks can be a problem – in which case, you could either turn

them inside out or source seamless socks, which can be found online.

- *Tight or loose clothing.* Do you have a preference? For some people, only really tight clothing will suffice, while for others, loose clothing is the order of the day. Sometimes there needs to be a certain level of pressure on a specific part of the body (e.g. the cuffs of a shirt need to be tight).
- *Belts.* Do you feel a strong need to wear one? Sometimes it can be of immense comfort to wear a tight-fitting belt. For some who find it difficult to automatically know where they are in relation to both themselves and others, a tight belt (for example) can give the wearer a better physical sense of self.
- *Buttons.* Like or dislike? Again this is a bit of a love/hate scenario! Some people find any unevenness in clothing a huge distraction or even painful, while others might love having certain types of buttons.
- *Shoes.* Is it easy or not to buy new shoes? Do you like to take your shoes off whenever possible? What about socks – are there similar issues? This is such a common one – very often, shoes (and socks) and autistic feet do not go well together. New footwear in particular can be difficult to find and get used to. Some people I know buy several pairs of the same style of shoe at a time, as they know that they can cope with them, and store them for future use.
- *Colour.* Do you have a reaction to certain colours of clothes? Sometimes the colour and/or pattern of clothes (your own and others') can significantly affect your emotional state. Some people gain high levels of positive energy from bright, multi-coloured rainbow clothes, while others need plain clothing. It's not uncommon for adults to be offended by certain colours and to find they simply cannot bear wearing them.
- *Hats.* Do you like to wear one? Sometimes autistic adults can't function 100 per cent unless they have a hat on. For some, this is because they need to feel something on their head in order to be comfortable. It is important to note that if you do have this need, then it's likely that there is a very good sensory explanation for it.

- *Trousers/shorts*. Do you have a preference? Some individuals will report that touch against certain parts of their bodies is painful. Some adults, for example, can only tolerate shorts, as the feeling of fabric against their knees is intensely painful.
- Do you have an apparent lack of ability to *dress appropriately to the weather*? Some people simply don't feel temperature in the same way as others – and the need to wear the same attire can lead people to wear clothes that seem inappropriate to the weather – e.g. shorts and a T-shirt in the depths of winter.

Do you have issues with any of the following?

- *Skin on skin contact*. Sometimes this can be unbearable. Wearing gloves and the like can be very beneficial.
- *Brushing past people*. This kind of 'light touch' can be problematic for some. Sometimes wearing a heavy coat or similar can reduce the level of discomfort. In addition, there are now companies who make specific undergarments that can be worn to reduce the impact of touch; some people find this of real benefit.
- *Proximity to other people*. You may find that you are accused of standing too close to someone, or too far away. If your proprioceptive sensory system is not helping you automatically judge distance, then you might need to consciously work out where to stand.
- *Hugs*. Do you like them or not? Do they need to be done a certain way? Sometimes hugs can be a source of great stress. That level of proximity to another person might be intensely uncomfortable. Sometimes hugs are OK as long as the 'correct' level of pressure is applied; sometimes they are OK if you are well prepared in advance.
- *Soft touches v. firm*. Do you have a preference? Again, a clear preference for firm touch over soft is quite common in my experience. A light touch can be horrible to endure for some, while deep pressure can be a source of great comfort.
- *The texture of food*. It might be that the texture is what you like or dislike about a certain food and the taste has nothing to do with it!
- *The shape of food*. In a similar way, the shape or colour of food, or whether different food groups are touching, might all influence

your eating habits. Try not to take it to heart if people accuse you of being a 'fussy eater' – there are very good reasons why you need to avoid certain sorts of food.

The next section, which relates to pain, is sometimes difficult for the PNT to understand or accept. Based on the personal reports of autistic individuals, as well as the multitude of autobiographical accounts and self-published writing (e.g. blogs), this section identifies that pain is clearly – for some – processed in a different way from most.

Do you show extreme hypersensitivity, for example to others touching the following?

- *Hair*. There are plenty of individuals who report discomfort when having their hair touched, washed, brushed or cut. In extreme situations individuals will report pain when confronted with any of these actions. This must be taken very seriously, however hard it is to understand (or even believe).
- *Nails*. Having your nails cut might be a painful experience. Sometimes it helps to file them instead, or make sure they are soaked to soften them first.
- *Teeth*. Plenty of people appear to have highly sensitive teeth, and can only tolerate certain toothbrushes. Going to the dentist might be an inordinately stressful (and painful) experience for you.
- *Deep pressure*. As described extensively by Temple Grandin (an autistic adult who has written books about her experiences) among others, deep pressure can be of benefit to some people. This *must* be very carefully considered though – it will not be to everyone's taste! However, deep pressure, along with small, enclosed spaces, wrapping oneself up tightly in blankets and the like, can be gorgeous experiences for some people.
- *Water*. Some people will hate the feel of water. Others may love it, but only in certain ways. For example, you may hate having a shower but love having a bath. You might love running water but find that motionless water stresses you out.

Auditory

Do you show intense hypersensitivity to a specific noise, such as the following?

- dogs barking
- paper tearing
- vacuum cleaners.

Do you have an inability to separate sounds, for example:

- *Background noise.* If you can't 'block out' background noise, then being in a busy environment can cause huge difficulties in terms of listening to any specific sound. Sometimes all the noise gets blended together to the point where you are unable to differentiate between sounds.
- *Voices.* If more than one person is speaking at the same time, then you may hear all the words together, as opposed to differentiating between the speakers. In a similar way, if there is a distracting noise (e.g. a clock ticking), this might affect the ease with which you can listen to and process what someone is saying.
- *Do you hear noises that others cannot?* You may have an extraordinary ability to hear sounds (including those of different pitch and frequency) compared to others. You may be able to hear the TV with the volume off, for example, or hear the electricity running throughout the house.
- *Do you love certain noises and seek them out?* Sometimes only certain sounds will do – and you might find yourself craving them. This might be a piece of music, or even a certain person's voice. On the flip side there may be certain noises that you simply cannot bear, and that are actually painful to you.
- *Do you tune into certain noises and then appear not to hear anything else?* You might find that if you are in the presence of a certain noise then it shuts out all other noises. This might be a good thing, or it might not!

Olfactory

- *Do you use smell to recognize objects or people?* Sometimes it's the smell of a person or object that will allow you to recognize them rather than using visual clues.

- *Is there extreme hypersensitivity – e.g. the ability to pick up smells that others cannot?* Some people are able to pick up the smells of certain things from extreme distances, or in tiny doses. So, for example, if you are hypersensitive to coriander, you will know if even the tiniest amount has been used in a meal – and this may be enough to put you off.
- *Are some smells overpowering?* Sometimes smell can be over-whelming in and of itself. The smell may not be bad, but you will find that you process it in an extreme way so that all your other senses are obliterated. For example, if someone wearing perfume is standing close by it might mean that you are unable to function until she has moved away.
- *Are certain smells greatly offensive?* You may have a very low toler-ance level to specific types of smell; if this ties in with a highly sensitive olfactory process then this can put you at quite a disad-vantage! I know someone who cannot bear the smell of a certain perfume and is able to sense it in a swimming pool, which means he can't subsequently swim there.
- *Do you seek out certain smells?* A great source of comfort for some are specific smells that reduce anxiety and can be carried around with you. Sometimes this might be a specific perfume or after-shave, or it might be something like lavender – each to their own!

Taste

- *Do you use taste to recognize objects or people?* In a similar vein to smell, you might be able to differentiate between people by their taste!
- *Does food need to be prepared in a certain way?* Many autistic indi-viduals are extreme in their eating preferences, in that they either seek out extreme tastes (e.g. very spicy food) or cannot bear 'taste' (e.g. they can't eat anything other than the blandest food).
- *Do you insist on eating or drinking certain brands?* You might be able to taste the sometimes extremely subtle differences between brands – e.g. you can only tolerate one brand of tea.

Visual

- *Do you notice patterns in your surroundings?* You might be one of those individuals who, without trying, notices patterns in their surroundings. These may be numerical patterns, or other patterns such as those in words.
- *Do you notice detail that others do not?* Some autistic adults are able to see the tiniest detail that others simply will not pick up on. This can be a really useful skill, but it might also mean that you are less likely to process the 'bigger picture'.
- *Do you like order?* For example. straight edges – darn that crooked picture! Other examples are being irritated by empty plug sockets with the switch turned on, tables pushed together without being 'properly' lined up, or books arranged unevenly on shelves. Suffice to say some people find such things so distracting that they cannot concentrate until the offending sight has been rectified.
- *Do you rearrange the environment to suit your own needs?* This can be a 'must' for some people; sometimes the colour of the wall must be a certain specific shade, for example. Other examples include being in an environment that is extremely uncluttered, although others may find it very bare, or having to line your pillows up in a specific way to allow you to feel comfortable.
- *Do you get absorbed in looking at certain things?* Sometimes you might become absolutely absorbed without realizing it, or without meaning to. For example, you may be distracted by TV or computer screens, or by a certain sight out the window. This can be both a positive and a negative – for some, it can be of great sensory comfort, while for others it can be a source of frustration.
- *Do flickering lights or screens bother you?* A common example often used by people trying to identify sensory differences is that of the fluorescent light; some will be able to see the flickering of the light, and it can be unbearable.

Vestibular issues

Your vestibular sensory system helps with things like balance. A hypo-sensitive vestibular system might drive the desire for certain types of movement which can be a source of extreme comfort. These movements may be more apparent at times of extreme emotion, whether positive or negative. So you might enjoy a lovely hand flap when excited about something, or feel the need for a really good rock when you're anxious. My view is that movement is extremely important to you, and that whenever and wherever possible autistic adults should be able to move about in ways that suit their individual vestibular style.

Some things that can be fantastic for those with vestibular needs include trampolines, hammocks, roundabouts and rocking chairs.

Proprioception

- Do you misinterpret how much to flex or extend your muscles when doing tasks?
- Do you struggle with your handwriting?
- Do you frequently break things by accident?
- Do you miscalculate weight?
- Do you use too much force, e.g. slamming doors or banging objects on to the table?
- Do you tend to bump into people when walking, or veer off from a straight line?
- Do you love deep pressure, e.g. strong hugs?
- Do you seek small, enclosed spaces?
- Do you walk on tiptoes?

All the above characteristics may indicate a difference in your proprioceptive sensory system compared to the PNT. And they all need to be taken seriously by others. For example, handwriting can cause considerable pain for some people – so why try and enforce it? In this day and age, touch typing is a far greater skill to have than neat handwriting.

These, then, are some of the things you might want to consider when understanding your sensory profile. It may well be that changing the environment in which you find yourself can alleviate some of the less favourable components of sensory experience, which can only be a good thing!

7

Diagnosis, identification and understanding of self

Let's start off by thinking about getting rid of the term diagnosis, shall we? I think a far better term is 'identification'. Generally speaking, the route towards being 'officially' identified plunges head-first down a heavily medicalized route, usually via a GP referral. I worry about the kind of message this gives you right from the outset. Most of us associate going to the doctor with being ill, or with having our symptoms identified to ascertain what is wrong with us and how it can be fixed.

If this is your mindset when it comes to autism, then straight away you are in potentially dangerous waters. Being autistic does not mean that there is anything wrong with you. You are not ill. You are not disordered. You are not impaired. Being autistic means that you are not part of the PNT; this does not make you a lesser person in any way. You don't need fixing. And you don't have symptoms! I am well aware that, for various reasons, being autistic can be hugely problematic for many people – but equally I am aware that many autistic adults fare extremely well and have happy lives; therefore, it is absolutely wrong to declare that all autistic individuals face problems as a direct result of being autistic. The number of people who go to a clinician to be told 'there's nothing wrong with you' is sinful; the individual is seeking an autism identification, and being autistic does not mean that there is something 'wrong' with a person.

I am not a clinician. I can't identify (i.e. diagnose) people as autistic, but I can, and do, have quite strong feelings about the pathways that people go down to gain an identity. I don't think that medical definitions based on an impairment model are healthy for autistic individuals. Nor are they healthy for parents, partners, employers – indeed, for society in general. To have to see a consultant via a GP referral, to sit in a waiting room, to be 'assessed' in a formal clinical environment, often by someone you have not met before – often with a heavy reliance on the things you might struggle with – all these things, consciously or otherwise, perpetuate the notion that being autistic is somehow being lesser. This may have major implications for the way you view yourself further down the line when coming to terms with the fact that you're autistic. If at every step of the way the identification is based on negative value judgements, then the concern is that this is how you may feel about yourself as a person long after the identification process.

At present there is no autism 'test' that will give you a definitive yes or no answer. Problematically, some sets of criteria include a reliance on observable behaviour – and yet one of the few things we know about autism is that there is no such thing as 'autistic behaviour'. In other words, there is no single behaviour or set of behaviours displayed by the autistic person that can't be seen in the PNT – if there was, then identification would be easy! This, then, makes a mockery of the idea of 'symptoms' or 'traits'. Certain behaviours *are* commonly associated with autism – in other words, many (but not all) autistic individuals display them – and yet these are not exclusive to the autistic population either. So saying that a person has 'autistic traits' could be seen as essentially meaningless.

But then comes the troublesome notion of whether autism even exists. If we can't 'see' it, or definitively identify it, then can autism be identified and applied to a population? My view is that autism absolutely exists as a neurological variance; autism is, relative to the PNT, a differing cognitive style and a different way of processing information within the social, communication and sensory domains, which significantly affects an individual's way of interpreting and experiencing the world. Autistic individuals differ from the non-autistic population in qualitatively significant ways, and it's our understanding of those differences that allows us to understand subsequent behaviours. Some might argue that that's all very well, but everyone is different; others might say we're all part of the same human race. I would agree with both, while still maintaining that the autistic population *can* be identified under the autism umbrella and *is* different from the non-autistic population, and that individuals have the right to be identified and understood as autistic people. For me, it's all about understanding groupings, levels and individuality. A simple parallel might be to think about dogs (I am not comparing autistic people with dogs – this is to demonstrate a concept only):

Are all dogs, dogs? Yes.
Can we categorize different types of dogs? Yes.
Are all dogs individual? Yes.

So, we are clear in our understanding and acceptance that all dogs are different, but we can label them all as dogs while having subcategories that define different breeds and so on. We understand and accept that within the dog population we *can* group types of dogs together while still recognizing the individuality of each dog, and that they all come under the collective term of dog. In a similar way, I would argue that while we are all part of humankind and we are all individuals, we can categorize groups within the population and it is helpful to do so.

Why do I think it's helpful? Here are some reasons:

- it enables others to understand you;
- it enables you to understand yourself;
- it explains certain reactions;
- it helps to reduce discrimination;
- it helps to reduce harmful labels.

The concept of viewing individuals 'through the autism lens' is a useful one. Understanding why someone might behave in a certain way can help provide explanations that otherwise would remain hidden – and, in many cases, without an understanding of autism harsh judgements and incorrect assumptions will be made. Some people argue that 'autism is a label', implying that that is a negative; my counter-argument is that without a correct identification you will be far more likely to be attributed a host of other negative labels that are often completely inappropriate. Rude, arrogant, aloof, insensitive, unfeeling – these are just some of the labels that have been applied to autistic individuals by people who have not understood how to view them through 'the autism lens'. Here are some examples based exactly on those labels:

Rude

'Excuse me, Miss, but why are you still so fat?' This was a question posed to one of his teachers by an autistic child in a mainstream school. She was extremely offended and the child was in line for a temporary exclusion.

Through the autism lens: the teacher had previously given a lesson in which she was teaching about health and nutrition. Within the lesson she had used herself as an example of someone who was overweight; she had been explaining about the correlation between healthy eating, exercise and body shape. Again, referring to herself, she told the class that she intended to lose weight by going on a diet and starting to exercise, and she stated that her body shape would change as a result. It was a few weeks later that the autistic child posed the aforementioned question. The reality was that the teacher had not managed to achieve her goal, and was, subsequently, 'still fat'.

When discussing this with the child his argument was that he had been doing exactly as he'd been told – he maintained that the teacher had stated, very clearly, at the beginning of the school year that if anyone in class didn't understand something within the lesson, then they should ask for clarification from her. His understanding was that the teacher was going to lose weight, and he was confused, as the evidence seemed to show otherwise – so all he was doing was asking for clarification *as directed by the teacher herself.* So, on the one hand, the teacher thought the child was being rude; on the other, he was an extremely conscientious and obedient student. The way in which he approached the problem may be deemed inappropriate – but there was no malicious intent, and certainly no rudeness involved.

Arrogant

'I suppose you think you're better at that than me?' Autistic response: 'There is no "suppose" about it, I'm definitely better at it than you.'

Through the autism lens: although he was speaking to his line manager at work the autistic employee saw no reason not to respond in this way. It's a simple case of weighing up the evidence

– and, in this case, the evidence demonstrably showed that he was, in fact, better than his line manager. He was not being arrogant, he was very simply stating what he saw to be factually accurate in response to a simple question.

Aloof

A husband is distressed because when his autistic wife gets home from work she never asks him how his day has been, never tells him how her day has been, doesn't even acknowledge that he is there – she goes into the bedroom and closes the door, shutting him out, leaving him on his own, and doesn't come out for at least an hour. Then she acts as though nothing is wrong.

Through the autism lens: she works in a busy environment in which she has to interact with several people during the day. By the time the working day is finished she is so exhausted by having to engage with people she simply has no energy left to be with anyone else. She loves her husband so much and can't wait to spend time with him, but she needs at least an hour to herself when she gets home to build up her energy levels, so that when she sees her husband she isn't an exhausted wreck.

Insensitive

In response to a friend disclosing that her brother had died unexpectedly, an autistic adult asked 'Did you like him when he was alive?' The friend was absolutely mortified at how someone could be so insensitive as to ask such a question.

Through the autism lens: the autistic adult was horrified that he could have caused any distress to his friend – he is, in fact, an extremely sensitive man who strives hard to be as kind and thoughtful as possible. His question was a genuine one to help him understand the level of support that might be needed. His logic was that if she hadn't got on with her brother then there was no real issue – but if she had been very close to him then he would have to carefully consider how he could provide support. The question was a simple fact finder, ironically as a result of how sensitive he felt towards his friend.

Unfeeling

Following the death of his mother an autistic adult threw himself into the funeral arrangements, organizing things down to the finest of details, but displaying no emotion although his wife knew that he had been very close to his mum.

Through the autism lens: the reality is that he was so swamped with emotion that he was unable to even begin to display it. His only way of coping was to focus on the practicalities; if he opened himself up to the emotional overload he would simply not be able to function. His lack of emotional display was a survival technique.

Why can't I get recognized as autistic?

We know very well that many people are identified as autistic only in adulthood – and we also know that many of those have struggled to get such an identification. We know too that plenty of people are absolutely certain that they meet the diagnostic criteria and yet they can't seem to get a clinician to understand them. The following are some of the reasons for this that I am aware of.

Masking

This was covered in Chapter 4 – but perhaps it's worth reiterating here. As I have already noted, autistic individuals tend to copy others or mask when they are anxious about how they might otherwise 'present'. And anxiety is often perpetuated by an unfamiliar environment, and when the individual has to engage with unfamiliar people, in an unfamiliar activity with very little predictability. I wonder if most 'diagnostic' assessments fulfil precisely these four criteria? If so, it may well be that the autistic adult almost automatically falls into her default masking persona – and thus does not present her 'true' self.

In addition, many autistic adults have been told frequently throughout life that their way of behaving is 'wrong'. They are told not to flap, not to hum to themselves while in deep thought, not to do all the lovely things that are fun and comforting – and, often, the reinforcement is that if they really have to do these things then they should do them in private and not in front of anyone else. It's all too easy for individuals to start to feel negatively towards their own behaviour; you are told you are in the wrong, or that you should behave in the way that comes naturally to you only in private behind closed doors. Imagine the level of shame that can start to creep in, the low self-esteem, and the culmination of it all – forcing oneself to present in an unnatural and forced way. This may be a seriously tough habit to break, and as an adult you will have been doing it for years. So is it any wonder that the individual may find it nigh on impossible to be his or her 'true self' in such a situation?

Not knowing what to say and what not to

In a similar vein to the above, many autistic people are told throughout their lives that they are 'too honest' – which to many autistic people is an oxymoron. However, they may have learned that when they tell the absolute truth they are frequently admonished for it. It is very difficult, then, to really know what is acceptable to say, and what isn't – particularly when the questions being asked may well be based on social convention and the like, which can be a source of confusion to the autistic adult. Again, the end result may be that the assessor fails to gain a full picture of the individual.

Fear of being judged

Some autistic people will be hugely anxious about disclosing the way in which their mind works for fear of being negatively judged for the way in which they think or behave. Again, being told throughout childhood and learning the hard way through experience can reduce the chances of the individual feeling comfortable in discussing his or her thoughts, feelings and behaviour.

Having an excellent understanding of autism

This might sound really odd – but it can be the case that an individual's own understanding of autism can be a hindrance to getting identified. Some adults will do huge amounts of research prior to seeking an assessment – but may then worry that the assessor will think that they are somehow manipulating them to give a 'diagnosis', and therefore will not disclose as much as they could. A similar analogy is the very bright individual who deliberately doesn't answer all the questions in his exam correctly because he is worried that the invigilator will think he must have cheated. Some autistic adults have done a similar thing in their assessments for fear that the assessor may think they are 'cheating'.

What can't autistic people do?

Some individuals have reported that they have been refused an identification because they have done something that, apparently, 'autistic people can't do'. I don't pretend to understand this. I have spent a huge amount of time and energy thinking about whether a sentence starting 'Autistic people cannot . . .' can be completed in a way that is subsequently valid and accurate for all autistic people. In other words, trying to find something that is fair to say to people as justification for them *not* being autistic. I came up with 'Autistic people cannot not be autistic' – which I think is absolutely valid and accurate, but doesn't really help in this context. I have made it quite clear that I believe autism to be a way of processing and thinking – and therefore, there *is* no behaviour that can be displayed that would warrant a negative identification. Some of the (extraordinary) reasons I have been made aware of by adults who have subsequently got a clinical diagnosis from a different professional include being told that the person can't be autistic because she or he:

- made direct eye contact
- had a good job
- was a parent
- was in a relationship
- had a lot of friends
- was female
- answered a direct question
- was dressed appropriately
- had an imagination.

Understanding of self – post identification

While this is the last section of the chapter, it may well be the most important. Without a good understanding of self, it is highly unlikely that individuals with autism will be effective at making choices that are beneficial to them. This relates very much to an understanding of how autism affects the way in which one lives one's life, and what needs to be taken into account in order to achieve one's goals. Essentially, making good choices depends very much on how well one understands oneself – and if you didn't realize you were autistic then a whole new understanding of yourself might need to be acquired somehow.

If an autistic person does not know that he or she is autistic (or, if she knows she is but does not understand what this actually means), then that person will often 'judge' herself against criteria that are not applicable to her. For example, a young autistic person may be told that 'everyone should have friends', and if she subsequently judges herself as somehow 'lesser' than her peers because she *doesn't* want friends, she will be the one who suffers from low self-esteem. Compare this to the autistic girl who knows full well the reasons behind why she doesn't (yet) want friends, is totally accepting of this, and is fully able to recognize that while many people have extensive friendship groups, not having them herself is nothing for her to worry about.

A rather absurd analogy, but one that does have some element of parallel: imagine a world populated almost entirely by men; you, however, are a woman – but, crucially, no one tells you! You go through life being treated differently, but you never know why this might be. You are uncomfortable having a wee standing up against a tree (and you're really not very good at it); your voice refuses to deepen as a teenager; you look different from others and stand out. However, one day you are 'diagnosed' as being a woman – you read up on womanhood, you identify the few others out there and connect with them, and you begin to understand that many of the ways in which you 'judged' yourself no longer apply. While you are the same person as you were prior to 'diagnosis', and while you are still treated differently by others, all a sudden you have a reassuring rationale as to why this might be. Your self-esteem increases, and you no longer try (with little success) to wee standing up against a tree. Life is suddenly much better.

As stated, rather an absurd analogy. But maybe also a useful one. If one understands the example of 'tree-weeing' as a 'behaviour' then all of a sudden the analogy has quite a depth of meaning. After all, how many autistic adults are held back in so many ways by trying to conform their *behaviour* to adhere to a PNT presentation – as opposed to feeling justified in behaving in their own logical autistic manner?

The concept is that having an accurate self-identity is extremely important for the autistic adult. In order to reduce those painful judgements of self it might be helpful for the autistic adult to explore what autism means to him. Here are some key pointers from my perspective:

- Do not judge yourself in comparison to the PNT.
- But do not judge yourself against other autistic adults either.
- Develop your own set of parameters against which you can judge yourself.

What I mean by this is that, being autistic, you have a very different set of criteria against which to view yourself compared to the PNT. You no longer need to feel like a terrible person simply because you find so many things so much harder than most other people. All those times when you have been told you are rude may not be because you actually are rude – it may because you simply misread a PNT-based interaction. Of course, being autistic is not an excuse for being rude – but knowing the difference between being deliberately rude and making an honest autistic 'mistake' may mean that you judge yourself in an entirely different way.

So, not judging yourself against PNT criteria is one thing; but neither is there much point in judging yourself against other autistic adults. For the vast majority of people I know who have been identified, their first reaction is one of massive relief. So many things click into place, the world finally has some sensible answers, and the individual starts to understand herself in a different and far more positive way.

However, she then starts reading everything she can get her hands on. She is delighted when she starts an autobiographical account and feels connected with the author. But – hold on – this woman you are reading about can understand the body language of cats. This chap is fluent in numerous languages. This person can focus on a task for eight hours straight. This one can hear whispered voices from the house next door. He has a meltdown when a certain advert comes on. She has a first-class degree in pure mathematics. But you don't understand cats in the slightest, you struggle to understand your own language, let alone others, your attention span is approximately thirty seconds, you can't hear anything at all over the noise of the central heating, and you failed maths GCSE!

Panic begins to set in – are you really a 'proper' autistic person? Are you, in fact, a fraud? Of course you're not – but it can be easy to fall into the trap of comparing your autistic self directly with others. You do belong to the population known as autistic – but you are a unique human being who will differ in some ways from everyone else.

What appears to work well for some individuals is the development of a conscious cycle of questions that form part of your mental routine when making decisions. Being taught a set of questions to ask oneself prior to making a choice can not only be liberating, but can also help the individual reduce risk in social situations. It may be useful to teach the autistic individual to ask herself the following questions:

1 What impact will my behaviour have on others in the immediate future?
2 What impact might it have in the longer term?
3 What impact will it have on me?
4 Have I made sure, to the best of my ability, that I am behaving according to what I regard as an appropriate moral and ethical code?

'Behaviour' in the above questions can relate to almost anything. If I may use myself as an example, I am privileged to be asked to speak at various conferences, and long ago I made the conscious decision not to get 'dressed up' – for example in a shirt and tie. Prior to this I used to wear a suit and tie, in which I felt extremely uncomfortable, and subsequently my delivery was poor. On reflection, I realized that while it seemed that most people who spoke at conferences *did* dress formally, and while there seemed to be an unspoken expectation of this from delegates, it was not entirely necessary. In relation, then, to the above:

1   What impact will my behaviour have on others in the immediate future? *What I have found is that after an initial 'raising of the eyebrows' no one really seems to have any negative reaction.*
2   What impact might it have in the longer term? *As far as I am aware there is no longer-term impact.*
3   What impact will it have on me? *Crucially, I now feel far more comfortable – and, as a result, more able to focus on what I am saying rather than being concerned at the impression I am making in regard to my appearance.*
4   Have I made sure, to the best of my ability, that I am behaving according to what I regard as an appropriate moral and ethical code? *This is of equal importance – if I am being paid to deliver a talk, it is my moral and ethical duty to do so to the best of my ability. If I have to 'bend' a social rule in order to do so, after having taken the first three questions and answers into account, logic dictates that doing my job to the best of my ability supersedes the following of a fairly minor social code.*

The end result (this is a somewhat trite example, but the principle remains the same) is that I genuinely believe that I have made a decision, based on my existing knowledge – while being fully aware that I may need to change the decision if new 'information' comes to light – that first allows me to be as productive as possible, while second, and of critical importance, I don't have to worry after the event about whether it was the correct decision or not. Many autistic individuals will spend hours, days, months, even years ruminating over past (and future) events, agonizing over their own actions in order to ascertain whether they were 'right'. Employing the above system may reduce this constant rumination, while allowing the individual to continue to learn, develop, and reduce the risk of behaving in ways that may be deemed offensive or inappropriate.

This routine of continuously asking a set of questions can be somewhat laborious – but once one is used to it I think that it can be overwhelmingly positive. If an autistic person does not auto-matically take into account his or her effect on others, then doing so via a more conscious formal route can be extremely beneficial to all concerned.

Understanding of self should be supported as soon as possible. It may be useful for the autistic adult to 'buy into' the conceptual understanding of the critical position first that difference exists, second that difference does not equate to negativity, and third that being in a minority group and being different does not mean one is inferior. This may take a considerable length of time to accept, but by not fully embracing these concepts there is the ongoing danger that the individual may feel less favourable to his or her self.

Disclosure

Once an individual has been identified as autistic, he has to decide whether or not to shout the fact to the rooftops or to keep it entirely to himself. However, it is possible that neither option is the best. Of course, for some people, one of these options might be entirely appropriate – but it's certainly not the case for everyone.

When considering this issue, here are some things to take into account:

- *What's said is said.* Once you have made the disclosure you can't take it back. Some people might want to express themselves to the world – and many get huge satisfaction and a feeling of com-munity by engaging with other autistic individuals online, via social media, and by blogging. Some people feel that they have a responsibility to share their stories to support others. However, do be cautious. It's easy to do these things under a pseudonym, so that might be an option; going out to the world using your real name may be something you need to consider very carefully before taking that step.
- *Will people think of me differently?* This is a very important consideration. It may be that you *want* people to think of you differently – but it may also be that you don't. Plenty of people in the world have preconceptions of what it is like to be autistic, and if these preconceptions are incorrectly applied to you then you might find it very frustrating.

- *Being treated differently.* Telling someone you're autistic might mean that they treat you differently. This can be a huge positive – but it can be a negative. On a positive note, if that person understands you better and is willing to take the fact that you are autistic into account, it can be a wonderful thing. Being accepted for who you are can be an amazing gift, and very liberating. However, as above, if someone then starts treating you differently when you didn't want them to, it can lead to tension and stress.

- Not *being treated differently.* Sometimes you may think that disclosure will automatically lead to greater understanding and acceptance, which may then enable you to be more 'yourself'. However, if others do not buy into the 'real you' they may assume that you *should* continue to be the person you've always been – which in many cases is restrictive and painful. This can be a huge blow – to go through the major decision to disclose and subsequently for it not to be taken seriously can be heartbreaking.

If you are an adult who believes yourself to be autistic then you may well want to have that belief corroborated in some way. But the corroboration itself is up for debate, in that some people will say that you cannot claim to be autistic without a clinical 'diagnosis' while others will say that knowing one is autistic after having done extensive research on oneself is perfectly sufficient in terms of declaring one's autism (one can find numerous blog entries on this subject, including those on my blog site). I would suggest that 'each to their own' is a suitable approach – but do take into account disability discrimination laws and your legal position in terms of whether you seek a diagnosis or not. You may decide that it's safer to get a formal identification in order to be protected legally – or you may decide that this won't be necessary.

8

Academic study

Academic study is something that many autistic adults may not consider based on their experiences at school. Of course, not everyone will have had a difficult time at school – but plenty will. Some of the reasons why educational experience can be negative include:

- being bullied;
- being misunderstood;
- not being 'allowed' to learn in a style that suits you;
- knowing more than the teacher (but finding that this did not go down well with said teacher);
- poor communication, leading to failure (e.g. not having clear instructions for course work, leading to lower marks);
- the school's failure to take into account your sensory needs;
- having to engage in subjects that seem pointless and irrelevant;
- large classroom populations;
- having to study multiple subjects.

The list could be longer, of course – but the point here is that in theory these are all factors which hold potentially far less relevance within a higher education (HE) context. I'm not suggesting that university students won't face difficulties if they are autistic – but some aspects of life within HE are actually more autism-friendly than within school. Having the opportunity to explore a narrower field in greater depth, for example, may appeal enormously to the autistic brain. In fact, I believe that for some autistic adults, the higher they get in their educational 'career', the more suited learning is to their style. For some, doing a PhD which requires intense, in-depth study, often in a rather driven way, might be the best fit of all degrees for the autistic adult. Being supervised by a small team, all of whom have vast knowledge of a very specific subject area, and being given the autonomy to work on one's own for lengthy periods of time, will suit some individuals perfectly – and they may be the same people whom the educational system has previously failed. So, even if school has been a miserable experience, don't assume that the same will be the case within higher education.

Some of the things you might want to consider when applying to a university and when you're there include the following.

Where the university is and what it looks like

Location can be of fundamental importance to the autistic student. The environment can play a massive part in the success or otherwise of the student. The size of the buildings, whether there is more than one campus, public transport facilities, the ease of getting from one place to another, and how close the university is to one's support networks, might all influence one's decision as to where to study. Some people, for example, might find a huge, sprawling campus too overwhelming; others may love the anonymity that a large university might provide. Of course, everyone will have their own preferences, but it's well worth visiting the university and spending time there just to see how comfortable (or otherwise) you are when you're actually there.

Getting around is also important. You might want to find out whether your course is taught in more than one location; if so, are all the buildings autism-friendly? You may, for example, need to be taught in a room with natural light – in which case, if your course has been allocated basement lecture theatres then it may cause you a problem. If you need to travel between one campus and another, are you comfortable with public transport? And if not, is it easy enough to walk?

Accommodation

Another consideration is accommodation. Remember that reasonable adjustments (the term used in the Equality Act, referring to the university's responsibility for making such changes to working practices, environment, etc. as are appropriate in order not to discriminate against any particular person) cover a wide range of things, not just your academic study, so if you need a reasonable adjustment regarding accommodation then you may well be entitled to it. So, for example, if you have a need to live on your own in halls throughout your university life, then you might be able to successfully request it. Some students like to live either at home or nearby, so that they know that if they need it, support will be at hand.

To disclose or not to disclose

Once you have decided where you want to study, you have a decision to make regarding the application form. Do you disclose or not? This is something that you may need to think about in other contexts (e.g. employment), but you don't need to be consistent in your decisions. Even if you choose to disclose at university, it doesn't mean you have to subsequently disclose elsewhere. There are some very good reasons why one might disclose being autistic on a university application form, as the law states that the institution must then make reasonable adjustments to ensure that you are not discriminated against. Because there are no hard and fast rules which govern reasonable adjustments, it's sometimes very difficult to know what these might look like. However, the main point is that without a disclosure, it is far less likely that your autistic needs will be met.

What the course requires

This one is really important. Some courses *require* you to do things that you may not feel comfortable with, in which case the course may not be for you. For example, if you have to go on placement as a mandatory part of the degree, then you will need to take this into account. Make sure that you have a good understanding of which components of the course are mandatory before applying.

How the course is examined

Some people are far better at coursework than exams, others may love giving presentations or sitting oral exams. It may well be worth ascertaining how your degree will be moderated, in other words how work is to be presented and assessed. If you find end-of-year exams utterly terrifying, then a course with greater emphasis on coursework submissions throughout the year might be better suited to your needs.

What the course will lead to

It may not be possible to think too far ahead, but it is worth considering why you are choosing the course and what it might lead to once it has been completed. Some courses may be less attractive than others – but might lead to more attractive employment opportunities once they are over.

What is expected of you as a student

Sometimes students think that they need to act in a certain way, or behave differently, just because they are at university. Of course, there are some expectations that you will need to identify and fulfil – not least the academic requirements of the course. But it's also worth noting that you are you, and you will need to look after yourself in the best way you can. Just because the majority of people go out clubbing at the weekend doesn't mean you have to – if it's not 'your thing' then it is highly likely that there will be alternatives, and you may be surprised at just how many others prefer to do things their own way.

What can universities do?

Rather than listing the reasonable adjustments that universities might offer, I have instead put forward here some ideas that could be seen as potentially autism-friendly within university life. These are not necessarily suggestions that come under the institution's duty to make reasonable adjustments, but they may be worth consideration in terms of recognizing the potential needs of autistic students might have. In no particular order of importance, they are:

Identification

Some students may come to university without a formal identification of autism. In such cases, if the university can provide a clear pathway towards how its student can get an autism 'assessment', then it will benefit the student hugely.

Communication

All autistic students will likely have their own preference in terms of communication methods. Some may find using the phone really stressful, while others may only communicate effectively via email. If student support can ensure that they identify a student's communication preference and subsequently make sure that all staff comply, then it can make a considerable difference to the student. For example, a student may request that if a university staff member needs to contact her by phone, then a text sent five minutes prior to the call as a 'pre-phone call warning' would be useful.

Academic staff may need to understand that a student's communication style may differ from what they are used to. Some students may require tasks to be set in a written format giving greater detail of what the task entails; some may need to have access to lecture slides prior to the lecture being held; some might need to question the instructions in order to ensure that they are not misinterpreted. Whatever the communication need, academic staff will need to be aware of what is required of them to make sure the student is not at a disadvantage.

Assessment of need

It is vital that university staff have access to expertise to help them understand what their autistic students require in terms of reasonable adjustments. Students are individuals – and, as such, there cannot be a 'one size fits all' approach, nor even a range of approaches. Some students may require an adjustment that is unique to them; the real issue here is how those specific needs are identified in the first place. It can take a very experienced, knowledgeable and skilled assessor to work with the student to identify what needs she might have, in order to identify how the university can meet those needs.

Late room changes

A common problem at university is that the location of classes can change at the last minute. This may cause considerable consternation for the autistic student, who may be reliant on his timetable as part of his daily routine. Turning up to find a handwritten note on the door explaining that the class is being held elsewhere may cause considerable anxiety, and the student may then lose out on his teaching. One way of reducing anxiety regarding such late changes is to always have a contingency plan in place; for example, a responsible student could be allocated to redirect students on a one-to-one basis from the expected venue to the rearranged one.

General changes

In a similar vein, there will be unavoidable changes throughout a student's time at university. A tutorial might need to be postponed, for example. This is inevitable – so it might be good practice to discuss with the autistic student how best to prepare for such eventualities; a text message, for example, giving clear instructions as to what has changed, how it has changed, and any action that is required by the student might be enough to alleviate any anxiety that might otherwise be caused.

Where to sit in a lecture theatre/classroom

Some students find that the sensory environment can adversely affect their learning. The layout of a classroom, the level of echo in a lecture theatre, the type of lighting, whether the student can sit next to a window – these are just some of the plethora of things that might influence a student. One student, for example, might need to sit at the back of a large lecture theatre, as near to the door as possible, in order to feel that there is an 'escape' close by if needed. Conversely, another student might need to sit right at the front so there is not a big crowd between him and the lecturer, which may be overwhelming to have to look at. Yet another student might need to sit in plenty of space, without anyone next to her, in which case allocating an aisle seat and placing a 'reserved' sign on the adjacent seat may be all that is required.

Clarity about work requests

The clearer the instructions about the work expected of students the better. Instructions should be written, whenever possible, in unambiguous language, in other words in such a way that the risk of a student having to interpret them is minimized – unless, of course, interpretation is part of the academic requirement.

However, instructions can also be too explicit. This may seem contradictory, but it's worth ensuring that some 'instructions' are actually presented as 'guidelines'. For example, a word count may be given as a guideline, not as an exact expectation.

Clear submission deadlines

Autistic students may need to know from the outset of a course when work is expected to be completed. This may apply to the whole academic year, so if at all possible the student should be provided with a year planner including key dates.

A single point of contact

At university the number of personnel involved in a student's life can be overwhelming. Rather than expecting that they have to engage with a large number of people, it may be useful for some students to know that they have a single point of contact. Of course, it might be that subsequently they are redirected – but just knowing that their first point of contact is always the same person can be extremely reassuring for some autistic students.

Consideration of group work

Plenty of students will find group work problematic. Some autistic students find group interactions so stressful that they cannot cope with them; others will find that it's not necessarily the interaction that is difficult, it's having to rely on others to engage in work activities that the autistic student needs to be in control of. Some autistic students will complete all the work in a group rather than just their own component to make sure it is done in a way that suits them. If the course does not require mandatory group work then it may well be a case of providing alternatives for some autistic students.

Flexibility of expectations/variety of methods of moderation

Many universities believe that their role goes beyond the teaching of academic subjects, and will take responsibility for developing skills such as those that may help in life beyond university, for example in employment. So, a university might encourage students to present work in front of the rest of the class, as a 'lecture', in order to develop presentation skills. However, this may put some autistic students at a major disadvantage if the anxiety caused by having to present is such that they end up dropping out, or becoming ill. While the development of a wider skill set is important, to many autistic students it is more important to be able to get their degree while maintaining good mental well-being.

Universities might also be flexible as to how work is moderated. Taking the above example, if within a course students are moderated via a presentation, then the presentation might take a form that allows autistic students to be moderated in a fair manner that does not put them at a disadvantage. They might video themselves, for example, rather than presenting 'live', or write a visual presentation with a voiceover.

Alternatives to traditional freshers' week activities

Many traditional activities at the start of the academic year are designed to encourage students to get to know one another – which can be one of the more terrifying aspects of university life for the autistic student from the outset. Activities often involve a level of chaotic activity, alcohol, unpredictability and so on – in other words, they may not be particularly autism-friendly. If the university can provide a range of activities that includes more autism-friendly inductions, then the start of university life may be a lot easier for some autistic students.

Timing of appointments

If an autistic student has any kind of appointment – be it for an assessment of need, a tutorial, a meeting – ensuring that the time of the appointment is such that it is highly likely to be kept is excellent practice. In addition, knowing the likely duration of the meeting will help. One way of doing this is to give the autistic student the first 'slot' of the day – which means that there is less chance she will have to wait.

Clear guidelines for tutorials

One-to-one situations can be just as problematic for some students as group work; feeling 'in the spotlight', having to engage in reciprocal verbal interaction, feeling that they must 'perform' to a certain expected standard can all be highly stressful for some.

Alternatives could be considered; holding email exchanges rather than face to face tutorials, for example, might be an acceptable way forward. If a student is going to attend a tutorial, it may be necessary to identify exactly what she needs to do in preparation, and what to expect within the tutorial. This may allow the student to prepare herself, rather than having to cope with the unknown.

Don't make assumptions

While university students will have a certain level of academic ability, it is useful for staff to understand that the overall skills of their autistic students may vary considerably from one individual to the next. It is far too easy to assume that because a student demonstrates an excellent academic standard, the same person will be proficient in other areas of life – but this may not be the case for all autistic students.

Many autistic adults will be able to work to a good academic standard. Very often it's not the academic side of university life that causes the problem, so institutions must recognize that supporting an autistic student goes above and beyond academic supervision to allow the individual to reach his or her potential.

9

Employment

Relationships at work

The world of work is very often an unforgiving one for the autistic adult. Much has been written elsewhere on employment, so I will focus this chapter on the following areas:

- the interview
- team skills
- social expectations.

These will be covered with reasonable adjustments in mind – and what follows is an example of what can go wrong when such adjustments are not made.

Reasonable adjustments – what happens when they are not in place

Here's a real-life example: Eve is working – and has been for five minutes (like her colleagues, she starts work at 9 a.m.). A colleague walks in and says to Eve, 'It's chucking down with rain outside.' Eve gets up and walks out.

Eve rang me that afternoon in a considerable state of distress. She articulated what had happened and explained to me from an autistic perspective what had led to her walking out of her job. The following account summarizes what she said to me (she not only gave her permission to publish this, she actively wanted me to):

1 Her colleague was late – and therefore, in the strictest sense, fraudulent. Eve felt intensely uncomfortable knowing this.
2 As she was being distracted from work, Eve was now also fraudulent, being paid to do a job that she was now not doing.
3 Her colleague had stated that it was 'chucking down with rain outside'. Eve could not comprehend this: she could see out of the

window, so if she wanted a weather report she could check for herself; she could see that her colleague was wet, and was perfectly able to recognize this as an indication that it was raining; as she had no intention of going outside, the information was irrelevant; and where else would it be raining, if not 'outside'?

4 Eve was now in a considerable state of anxiety, but she also knew that it was socially expected that comments such as these required some kind of reciprocation.

5 What Eve really wanted to do was behave in such a manner as to get rid of her colleague as quickly and efficiently as possible; however, all she could think of doing was to punch her – and, knowing that this was not socially appropriate, she chose what she saw as her only other option, which was to leave. Eve was the one who lost her job. This was despite the fact that a reasonable adjustment had been identified which stated: 'Do not communicate with Eve during working hours unless it's specifically work-related'.

Going through the stages of employment, it might be useful to consider some adjustments that may make the autistic adult experience less stressful.

Job descriptions and person specifications

In this day and age it seems often to be the case that a job description is extremely generic – and that person specifications ask you to be good at pretty much everything under the sun. Obviously this is an exaggeration, but it is apparent that being reasonably good at a range of things seems to be preferable to having a specific skill but perhaps being not so good in other ways. This, one might argue, puts the autistic adult at a disadvantage straight away. One characteristic we recognize in the autistic population is a spiky skills profile – in other words, the ability to do certain things to a highly competent degree, while at the same time being very weak in others. It is often the case that people will make assumptions as to an employee's skill set, and the application of these assumptions to an autistic adult could well lead to disaster.

A simple example might be that of skill in communication. Most people recognize that communication is a two-way thing – there is expressive communication and receptive communication. Most people are reasonably similar in terms of their skill set in both categories; therefore, one might listen to an individual's level of expressive language and assume – usually correctly – that her receptive skill level is on a par with it. However, this may not be the case for the autistic adult. She might have an amazingly high level of linguistic expression, an ability to articulate to a splendidly high standard. But receptively, she may operate at a far lower level than one might expect. If job descriptions go down the 'Jack of all trades, master of none' route then one could argue, strongly, that autistic adults are being disadvantaged from the outset.

So what can be done?

Employers should be allowed – indeed, encouraged – to use their judgement when it comes to matching job descriptions and person specifications with a prospective autistic employee. Recognizing that some people's strengths seriously outweigh their weaknesses would not only increase employment opportunities for the autistic adult, it would also be an asset to the employer in many cases.

The interview

If one has applied for a job and been offered an interview, it is then that the fun begins. I do not intend to provide tips for how to be successful in an interview; rather, let's explore the notion of the interview to ascertain whether it is, in fact, a useful guide to a candidate's suitability for employment.

Why do most organizations interview people before employing them? To me, this is a highly pertinent question, and one which needs severe examination and scrutiny. How many people are excellent in an interview, but subsequently prove not to be any good at their job? How many people are so anxious during interview that they fail to get appointed, when in reality they may be excellent at the job they applied for? What relationship – if any – is there between being interviewed and doing a job? Unless the job itself involves 'being interviewed', then one could argue that the relationship between interview and ability to perform a job is tenuous, at the very least.

So, again, why do most organizations interview people before employing them? I don't know the answer, but I do know that the interview process can be so terrifying for autistic people that it severely decreases their chances of finding gainful employment. This is a massive blow, not just for the person with autism, but for organizations that may benefit from the qualities an autistic person could bring them if only he were given the chance. Of course, I am not suggesting that all autistic people are good employees, but I am suggesting that the interview process excludes many autistic people who *would* make good employees.

I once hosted an employment forum about autism and work; all the autistic participants said variants of the same thing – namely, that the best way to determine whether or not a person was good at a job would be to allow them to do it and judge them on their merits – be it doing the job for one hour, half a day or a week. At least it would seem a far fairer (and more realistic) manner of recognizing who would be best at the job. I can imagine employers shuddering at the notion that they should allow potential employees to do a job for a day to ascertain how good they actually are – but, in the long run, if that process is more effective than interview, reducing the possibility of employing someone who subsequently proves to be substandard, then it could be seen as an extremely positive way forward. Obviously, dependent on the job itself, some organizations would have to create a false environment in which to display candidates' work skills, but the concept itself remains sound.

What can be done here?

Even if an 'interview' is deemed to be an integral part of the process, we should ensure that a range of options are offered to any autistic adults on the shortlist. It might be useful to provide interview questions in advance (to all candidates, so as not to give anyone an unfair advantage); to offer written interviews, possibly even live online interactions to avoid overly stressful face-to-face encounters. It might be that a candidate has more specific requirements, such as needing to familiarize herself with the interview environment the day before, or needs to be interviewed first in order to avoid any risk of the panel running over time, which could cause some people dangerous anxiety and put them at a disadvantage.

Another issue when it comes to interview is that the PNT 'system' is so complicated to understand. Many autistic individuals find themselves 'punished' for being honest, for example. This works – oddly enough – in two apparently contradictory ways: first, one should not be too honest when one is extremely good at something, as this might come across as 'big-headed' or 'arrogant'; however, one must also be less than honest in identifying areas that one might not be so good at, as it may interfere with one's success at interview. Most successful PNTs will understand how to 'play' the 'interview game', while many autistic adults – who might be brilliant employees – might not. It would be wonderful if employers understood that their autistic interviewees are likely to need very specific, direct questions, and that their answers are likely to be less governed by 'interview convention' than those of PNT candidates.

Team skills

Let's get one thing straight – some autistic people will be far more effective at working on their own than being part of a team. If this is the case, why is it that they are often forced into a position that – literally – helps no one? If an employee can generate more output singularly than collectively, then surely sense should prevail and allow the employee to do just that. Sadly, this is not usually the case. More importantly, however, there seems to be a pervading societal acknowledgement that 'it is good to be part of a team' – although no one seems to be able to back this up with a rationale that's valid for everyone. For many with autism it is simply not the case – the stress of being part of a team may well be counterproductive for some people, in which case it is probably for the best to leave the 'team sentiment' to one side and allow them to get on with life in the manner that suits them (and, in all likelihood, the other members of the would-be team).

Sometimes, particularly in education – school, further and higher – teamwork is part of the curriculum. This is where 'reasonable adjustments' under the Equality Act might come in. If it can be demonstrated that making an autistic student work in a group puts him at a distinct disadvantage as a result of his 'disability' (I do not consider autism a disability, but this is the word used in law), then it may be appropriate to make reasonable adjustments, either by allowing the individual to engage in solitary activity, or to give him a very specific task that benefits the group without him having to take part in the group work itself. If a role requires team skills – as many jobs will – then it is important for the autistic individual to recognize this, and judge for himself whether or not the role is suitable.

Social expectations

Some jobs require high levels of PNT social skills; many, however, do not. I frequently encounter individuals who are struggling at work for reasons that have nothing to do with their skills in employment (i.e. doing the job they are paid to do). The problems arise from others' expectations that they should engage socially, even though doing so is not part of the job description. The pressure to chat – not just in breaks, or before or after work, but *while working* – or to participate in social activities (such as the dreaded Christmas party) can be daunting to the point of causing considerable stress to the autistic employee.

If an individual feels that he is being negatively judged – or if, more realistically, he *is* being negatively judged – by not wanting to (in the eyes of his colleagues) waste time on social interaction, preferring to get on with work, he may be the one who ends up suffering. In some cases it is the person who is dedicated to work and less inclined to use work hours socially who is the one with whom employees have an issue with!

Here is an employment scenario to consider:

Bob

Bob is a very serious, goal-oriented autistic employee who has a high degree of focus within his work and is attending a team meeting, for which he has been responsible for drawing up an agenda. As usual, Bob has meticulously emailed all those invited to the meeting to ask for their agenda items, and has calculated to the minute how long each item needs in respect of the duration of the meeting. In the meeting, however, Bob frequently has to interrupt people and say 'That isn't the current agenda item, please wait,' or on one occasion 'That isn't on the agenda at all, so we shouldn't be discussing it.' He also makes several remarks about when it is time to move from one agenda item to the next. None of this goes down at all well with his colleagues, who see the meeting as a time to discuss work-related matters in general, and in the past have not bothered to submit items for the agenda as they've simply brought issues with them to the meeting for discussion.

Through the autism lens: in a sense the problem here lies with the differing expectations of the different employees. Bob, from his perspective, is doing exactly what he believes his role to be. Everyone has had their chance to submit items for the agenda, he has spent considerable time and effort in drawing one together, and has gone over and above his duties in identifying the duration of each item. He is distraught at the lack of respect showed to him by people ignoring his carefully planned agenda and timings.

Through the PNT lens: Bob's colleagues are a laid-back group and have always taken an open-ended approach to team meetings; they have always felt that they could be open in meetings and discuss issues they felt were pertinent. They are annoyed with Bob's insistence that they submit agenda items, and distraught at the lack of respect he shows them by cutting them short.

It's pretty easy to see here just how quickly both parties' lack of understanding can end in a no-win situation. However, some very simple adjustments and a modicum of understanding both on the part of Bob and his colleagues would have decreased the risk of distress all round.

The following are some other common issues that might arise for autistic employees within a workplace:

The office environment

Some autistic adults simply cannot operate in an open-plan office, or an office with any level of unpredictability, or even in one with other people. From a sensory perspective alone it might be impossible to work effectively; over and above that, the increased chances of the need for social interaction, or even the possibility of it, might be too much for the autistic employee.

Telephones

Plenty of autistic adults cannot bear using the phone. Unless this is an integral part of an employee's role it is best to avoid putting pressure on her to use or have to answer the phone. Sometimes the individual can use the phone if she is the one in control – for example if she is the one making rather than receiving the call.

Breaks

If at all possible, support the individual to decide when and how to take any breaks he is due. It may well be that he chooses to have a break at different times from most of his colleagues – not only does this remove any need for social interaction, he then has some quiet time to get on with work when everyone else is on their lunch break!

Line management

Sometimes people are promoted because they are so good at their job, and their responsibilities subsequently extend to managing others. Some may enjoy this and be very good at it – but for others the skills required are so different from their natural skill set that they become anxious to the point of having to take time off for work-related stress. Line management is not for everyone – individuals should be matched with their skill set rather than having to follow a 'traditional' career pathway.

Apparent lack of flexibility

Some autistic individuals are very 'rules based', which may lead to apparent inflexibility in working time. For example, an employee may not understand that at certain busy times he may need to work longer hours than expected. Many of the issues related to this are caused by a lack of clarity as to expectations, rather than being any fault of the employee.

Poor understanding of autism

So many issues for autistic individuals at work stem very simply from a lack of understanding on the part of their colleagues and managers. Staff training and development might help in such cases but is not always the answer. Some people, it seems, simply cannot understand the autistic perspective – they are literally unable to empathize in any way with an autistic colleague. In such cases, is it fair on either employee to expect them to work successfully together?

Communication

Many autistic adults have a preference (or even a need) for absolute clarity in the directions and requests they are given; on top of that, many will have a preference (or a need) for clear *written*, as opposed to verbal, instruction. Giving written instructions that lay out clear expectations (e.g. time frames) for tasks at work can be a hugely beneficial way forward.

Sensory issues

I think that a full sensory assessment within the workplace could benefit autistic employees. Sometimes the sensory environment impacts negatively when it could be easily changed to meet the sensory needs of the autistic employee.

Self-employment

Some autistic adults take the logical step of becoming self-employed. Those who know they cannot comfortably exist in a world of work that makes intolerable demands decide to work for themselves and reduce a whole host of problems that come with being employed by a company or similar. Not everyone's skill set or vocation allows for this, of course, but for some people self-employment is a wonderful option.

Statistics suggest that the vast majority of unemployed autistic adults want to work, and there are very many excellent autistic employees. And yet statistics also show that the majority of those who want to work remain unemployed. It is reasonable, therefore, to suggest that there is still an awful long way to go before the needs of autistic adults are met within the employment arena.

10

Close relationships and parenthood

Love and relationships

What can be written about love and relationships in relation to autism? What we can probably acknowledge is that the myths perpetuated with regard to autism and relationships are just that – myths. It was with huge sadness that I heard of women not accessing an autism assessment for fear that by being identified as autistic they would be seen as inadequate or poor mothers. Why this would be the case is beyond me – I know plenty of autistic mothers who seem to me to be absolutely brilliant (particularly when their children are also autistic).

Even more bizarre, perhaps, is the notion that an autistic adult will never get to the point of being a parent. This is so obviously untrue that it seems odd to even have to put it in writing. An autistic person is as capable of love as anyone else; indeed, individuals often report to me that they believe that the intensity of their feelings appears to be far stronger than in the general population; this is not easy to quantify, but certainly feelings such as fierce loyalty and the willingness – even the need – to do anything they can on behalf of someone else can be readily identified in many autistic individuals.

For the sake of simplicity, here is a brief question and answer session. Can autistic people:

- love?
- have successful relationships?
- enjoy a happy sex life?
- have children?
- be good parents?
- make excellent friends?
- bring selflessness and compassion to a relationship?

The answer to all the above is an indubitable 'yes'.

Another question often posed is 'Is a relationship between two autistic people likely to be more successful than one between an autistic and a PNT person?' There is no answer to this, except that it all depends on the individuals in question. There is nothing to preclude success in relationships – some relationships work, some don't. Having noted that, there does need to be some acceptance by both parties of one another's differences in order for a relationship to be successful – but I guess that can be said of any relationship.

Similarly, does an autistic child have a better chance of good parenting if a parent is also autistic? Not necessarily – but it may be beneficial. There are pros and cons, and it again comes down to the nature of the two individuals. Equally, it is clear that PNT parents can be brilliant with their autistic offspring. What is important is the level of understanding on the part of the parent, wherever that understanding comes from – not whether the parent is autistic or PNT.

I have written the next part of the chapter as a series of mini 'stories', as the subject matter is something that many either find it difficult to discuss, or read about, or know how to go about finding useful information about. I hope you enjoy them. All the characters are writing from an autistic perspective. Their age does not matter. The subject matter of this chapter could easily fill a book in its own right, so please don't think I have touched on anything but a very few examples of what may be issues in a close relationship.

How do I know she fancies me?

She's stunning. She just looks so, I dunno. Just, right. Is she looking at me? How am I supposed to know? I don't look at people all that much anyway, too much information for these little eyes, so mostly I peep out of my peripheral vision; doesn't really help though, not when I'm trying to figure out if she's looking at me or not. What was it I read when I was trying to find out what clues to look for to identify if she fancies me? The list – where did I put the list? Got it. The list. Right.

So, number one: proximity. According to this, she'll stand close to me if she likes me. What? I mean, what? She's stood close to pretty much everyone, we're in a crowded students' union, how else is she supposed to stand? That makes absolutely no sense whatsoever; am I supposed to assume she fancies that girl she's always glued to at the hip just because she's stood real close? Or the barman, because he's the closest male? Well, it's certainly not me then, that's for sure. I am at least – by my approximate calculation – at least four to five inches further away than at least one other guy. No, I'm not having that – this proximity thing must be rubbish.

But not to worry – back to the list; thank goodness for the list. Conversation; she's supposed to be chatting with me and helping me along with the conversation with more questions than one-word answers. Oh. Right, well that's another no-brainer then, this place is far too loud to have a decent conversation in, so we may as well scrap that one. Bloody hell, this isn't as easy as I'd hoped.

Back to the list. OK, Hang on, what's this? She's going to touch me gently? No she bloody well isn't, not if I have anything to say about it. She can either touch me good and proper or get lost entirely. Everyone knows touching lightly makes me want to rip off their fingers and then scrub myself with a wire brush to get rid of the sensation. If she fancies me and tries on that lark she can think again. Oh, I'm getting nowhere here, might have to think about leaving. But I've only just got here . . . Persevere, young man – everyone else seems to work it out.

OK, get a grip and try harder! List, help me. Right – she might respond if I make comments to no one in particular. Excuse me, come again? Why would I ever make a comment to no one in par-ticular? I'm autistic, I'm not hallucinating and talking to no one! And I'm not at all sure I'd want to know someone if she randomly started chatting to strange men, apparently blurting things out to anybody with some vague hope that it will lead to marriage. Who wrote this bloody list?

Flipping of hair and dangling of shoes? Right, this list is getting seriously odd now. I'm not sure I actually trust it as much as I did ten minutes ago. Let's just have another scan . . . Reading her eyes – what the hell does that even mean? Why on earth would I do anyone the injustice of massively invading their intimate private space by looking in their eyes in the first place, let alone what I would 'read' even if I did? I mean, eyes are eyes, aren't they, not books? Reading of eyes? I mean, this world is strange enough without having to work out that cryptic nonsense. OK, I give up on this list. I'm just going to have to work it out as I go along, so here goes – wish me luck. Bother. She's gone.

I find the thought of kissing utterly repulsive

Dear Agony Aunt,

I don't know if I will ever pluck up the courage to send this but anyway I'm an autistic girl and I like boys. Sometimes, they even like me back. That's fine. I'm perfectly happy to be liked, and I do find the idea of having a boyfriend really comforting. Someone to be myself with, who can squeeze me when I want/need to be squeezed, who won't think I'm weird just because I like to curl up in my favourite colour jumper in my home-made den in the corner of my bedroom, who understands that I don't always feel like talking, who won't make me go to cinemas that are too loud and scary. I can cope with explaining these things, because I think they're just me, and if he can't understand that then he doesn't deserve me anyway.

No, my problem is bigger than that. It's this kissing thing. I just don't get it! Even the thought of it now makes me feel sick. Lips have their own very specific texture, you see, and that subtly changes depending on how wet they are. I find it hard enough to touch my own lips together – I really love disguising them by applying different flavoured lip balm, that helps a lot. But the idea of introducing my own hyper-sensitive lips to someone else's? That I just can't bear. What am I supposed to do? Am I the only person in the world who finds the idea of kissing utterly repellent?

What did I do wrong?

Not again. Why does it always happen to me? Why? I know I've done something wrong. I know it. I've learnt the hard way, I now know that her lack of speaking isn't an indication of having nothing useful to say, but because she's annoyed with me. When I ask her if she's OK and she gruffly states, 'I'm fine,' I know that it's not really true. I know this because in the past when I've taken it at face value, she's then told me at a later date that using 'that tone of voice' means that she means the opposite of what she's actually said. I mean, how does that work? What's the point of that?

Anyway, lessons learned and all that, so I know I've done something wrong, I just need to work out what. How far back do I need to start thinking? Good question. It's evening now. I'm pretty sure she was OK with me last night, so maybe I ought to go through today's events from the moment the alarm went off, just to be on the safe side. Yes, today from the alarm, that's what I'll do. And I'll need to carefully consider all my actions against what I can recall from past events when I've 'got it wrong'. I'll list all I can remember of things that had the potential risk of 'wrongness' and check the list off . . .

1 When the alarm went off I *didn't* leap out of bed and throw the curtains open. I know I'm not supposed to do that. Apparently, some people like to 'wake up slowly' – something I still can't get my head around. Surely you're either awake or you're not? And once you're awake you want to be starting on the day's activities, else it's time wasting. But no, I laid nice and still for at least five minutes, so it can't be that.

2 Did I remember to ask her if she wanted a cup of tea rather than assuming she did because I always have tea and used to assume everyone else would be the same? Yes, I did – because I remember having to make her a coffee.

3 Did I grumble about the disgusting smell of coffee in the house that lingered long after she'd drunk her cup? I remember that I mustn't go on and on about revolting smells that apparently don't offend others. No, I didn't grumble – I used that technique of going into the bathroom and venting my spleen to myself in the mirror to get it off my mind, I didn't grumble directly to her.

4 Did I get overtly annoyed at the mess she left after making breakfast? I don't think so. I think I remember forcing my face not to scowl, and I simply took everything out of the dishwasher and put it all back in the way things should go, not the haphazard and frankly crazy way she does it. She says it's irritating that I *have* to do it 'my way' and I've long since given up on trying to explain just why it should be done in a certain way to maintain

dishwasher efficiency and increase chances of clean dishes. So I don't think it was that.

5 I remember telling her to 'take care' when she went to work – even though it's absolutely a waste of words as far as I'm concerned. Who's going to respond to 'take care' with 'OK, I will. Lucky you said that because otherwise I was going to behave rather recklessly and wasn't going to take care at all'? Bit like those 'baby on board' stickers that make me want to politely tap on the window and declare 'Wow, so lucky I read that sign, sir. I was actually going to run into the back of your car until I realized that there was a baby on board' . . . but I digress.

6 I had the day off and she was at work. So, surely there can't have been anything I could have done or not done in that time. She wasn't even with me, so can I fast forward? I think so.

7 She came back – did I ask her how her day had gone? Yes. Did I listen to the response this time? Yes. So, not that either.

8 I made dinner so it can't be anything food related. I can't have commented on the amount of calories she'd consumed or commented on the impact they might have on her body shape – come on, I learned that lesson ages ago!

9 I give up. So, how do I handle it? I guess I'll just have to exist in a state of perpetual anxiety until either I discover what I've done wrong, or she actually tells me, or I die. This relationship stuff is so hard. Such a shame. I get told off when I tell people what they've done to upset me, but I think it's the sensible way forward, but then what do I know . . .

Next day, a text message from my gorgeous but tough to read partner: 'Sweetheart, I'm sorry for being off with you. It's just I find you so infuriating at times. You know when my mum rang when I was out at work? Do you recall the conversation? You told Mum that actually I *was* totally pissed off with her, that I was deliberately avoiding her calls and I thought her cooking was pants. Darling, when are you going to understand that when I tell *you* something, it doesn't mean you can tell the rest of the world? I'm so glad I've got you, but can you try a bit harder in the future?'

Back to the drawing board for me then, as always.

How can I make sex smell less obvious?

Sex stinks. I don't mean I don't like it or I'm bad at it, not at all. I mean it literally. It smells – and it smells really, really strong. On the one hand the sensations are pretty darn delicious, but then come the strong smells that seem to go with it all. And the more fun the sex, the stronger the smell. Trouble is, I find myself more and more wary of engaging with her in the bedroom and I can't tell her why. It sounds as though I don't like her as a person, and that's anything but the truth. I love her, I adore her, and I would enjoy the sex thing so much if she didn't, you know, smell – it's not even a bad smell, it's just so powerful that it's overwhelming. I wonder if I could get away with one of those nose things like they wear in synchronized swimming? But imagine the scene – 'Hang on love, I can smell you getting turned on, let me just pop this on my nose.' I don't know, but I suspect it might be a mood killer. But where in the world is the manual that tells me how to broach this particular subject? It's hard being me sometimes.

Will he think I'm weird?

I'm not weird. At least, not in my eyes. I think I'm one of the least weird people out there. Not according to almost everyone I've ever met, of course – but according to my logic and my way of under-standing the world, it's them that are the weird ones. Harmless enough, in the main, but pretty odd nonetheless. But I know that others do find me strange when they get to know me; and the more they get to know me the more odd things they seem to find out. Some of them I've listed here – and I'm going to write the list for him, so he can understand just why it's them not me who's weird . . .

1 I don't see the point in talking. I don't mean I never speak, just that the vast majority of what people say seems to me to be irrelevant. All my life I've been told I'm too shy, too quiet, too whatever – I'm not, I just only say things that really matter. I hope he understands that being quiet and not talking for me is an absolute delight.

2 I wear what I want to wear. I don't understand what any occasion has to do with what I'm 'supposed' to wear. Clothes are because

it's not deemed polite to walk around starkers, and to keep me warm. Anything else is a bonus – so, for me, always wearing dark colours that are tight on my legs and loose on my top are perfect. I get accused of wearing the same thing all the time, which is ridiculous. I have at least five pairs of black leggings at any one time; they are clearly not the same pair that I wear over and over again. I'm told I'm boring and wear 'depressing' clothes – as if clothes can be depressed! I can tell you, I've yet to meet a jumper that looks down in the dumps . . . unless people mean that the clothes are what make me depressed, in which case they need to seriously re-evaluate their world view over what causes depression.

3 I tell the truth. OK, this one really is weird. Apparently, telling the truth is not what you're supposed to do – despite parents and teachers telling me all my life that it is exactly what I am supposed to do. If he asks me something, I'm liable to answer it truthfully – even if this isn't 'correct'. I suppose it's up to him then to only ask things he wants the answers to!

4 I don't buy presents when I'm 'supposed' to. What is it about society that dictates that we're supposed to buy presents on birthdays, for example? I can't handle it at all. The pressure is such that my mind goes completely blank. The plus side is that I love buying things as and when I see them or think of them – eminently more sensible in my view.

5 I'd like to plan sexual encounters, please. OK, I accept that this one does make me stand out – but surely it's sensible to know when to expect a sexual encounter so that one can prepare emotionally, mentally and physically for it? I'm a happy negotiator – we can bargain as much as you like, so long as we come up with a mutually agreed week-by-week diary of when, where, and how we intend to embark on those fun parts of being together.

6 Last, but not least, can you leave me alone, please? How people can bear to be together, seemingly without a break, is beyond me. But don't take it personally when I've just had enough and need some alone time; don't assume that because I can't be with you right now it means I don't love you. Believe me when I explain that my need for solitude has nothing to do with my feelings for you. OK?

Romance isn't dead

Some of the most romantic people I've ever met are autistic – so if you buy into the myth that autistic people don't ever do romance, then think again. The woman who bought a Hoover because her husband insisted on referring to the vacuuming as 'hoovering' despite the fact that they had a Dyson – I think that's amazingly romantic. Rather than get annoyed and insisting he change his incorrect terminology, she solved the problem so both of them could be content. The man who told his wife, who was worried about putting on weight, that he was absolutely fine with her being fat as there was more of her to love; and, anyway, that fat feels so much lovelier to stroke than skinny bits of the body. It may seem unconventional, but it's romantic nonetheless. In fact, I think autistic adults make so many unnoticed sacrifices for their partners that much of the romance is in doing exactly that.

Being a parent

I'm next going to explore various issues of being a parent. Very many autistic parents will have similar issues in relative terms to their PNT counterparts, but there may be some other issues that it is useful to consider. Therefore, this section may come across as more negative than others in the book – this is because I have drawn attention to some of the problems that might be associated with being a parent, as opposed to simply celebrating how wonderful it can be for anyone.

This section does not discriminate between genders – aside from the obvious bits, it's is aimed at both parents – Mum *and* Dad. The issues will not affect all autistic parents in the least, and they are not given in any particular order.

Finding out

Plenty of autistic individuals really, really don't like unexpected news. If you are planning a baby and one begins to make itself known, all well and good; however, when it is unexpected the feelings that you might go through can be complicated and, let's face it, even frightening. Change is something that you might find difficult – and having a baby is one of those things that definitely mean change is going to occur. Rather like puberty, change at this stage is inevitable. In order to counteract any feelings of anxiety that come with the prospect of imminent change you may want to find out as much as possible in order to prepare yourself. Which again is a problem, because . . .

Not a lot can be predicted

The course of events during pregnancy and beyond is highly unpredictable – and, as a result, fairly autism-unfriendly. The majority of births, for example, do not happen on the predicted due date. As an autistic adult this may cause you considerable consternation. To start with you won't even know what sex the baby is – but at least it can only be one of two . . .

All sorts of new things in your life

All a sudden life is very different from what it used to be. You may find that you have to change your lifestyle, your sleeping patterns, your day-to-day activities. Over and above that, you will need to meet medical staff, perhaps go to classes, and mingle with strangers – all of which can be stressful. Other things change, too. For the bearer of the baby there may be hormonal changes which cause mood fluctuations; this can be tough, both for you as an autistic woman and tough for your autistic partner, who may find the unpredictability stressful.

Invasion of privacy

What is it about having a baby that seems to mean you are no longer allowed your own space? People seem to think dropping in to see your baby is perfectly reasonable, strangers approach you in public to tell you things you already know, like what a beautiful baby you've got. For many autistic individuals, actually having a baby and all the issues associated with looking after it is not the most problematic aspect – it's the increased contact with others that can cause a great deal of the stress.

Social contact

One of the major changes that being a parent can lead to is unwanted interaction with people who would otherwise never be a part of your life. This isn't always a bad thing – you may make friends as a result – but sometimes it can be a painful reminder why you have gone through life being very careful who you expose yourself to socially. Suddenly, you're doing the school pick-up and it's fraught with danger. You can be spoken to at any time, by anyone. It seems that the school playground is an arena where social conventions are different from those that apply almost anywhere else. It's as if it is a 'free for all' where anyone has permission to speak to anyone else. Stressful indeed.

Then there are the parties: the invitation to your daughter to come to a birthday party and the expectation that you stay and chat with the other parents. The parents' evening where you're expected to engage with teachers. The myriad of social events that prior to being a parent you didn't even know existed. Of course, some of these social events can be avoided – but, sometimes, they are a necessary part of being a parent.

False accusations

Warning: this is not fun to read . . .

In a number of cases I am aware of, an autistic parent has wrongfully been accused of bad parenting. Safeguarding issues have been raised, or the parents have even had the child (or children) taken away from them. Very often (but not always) the parent is undiagnosed and equally often the children involved are also autistic. In each case where it has come to light that the accusations are false, it seems apparent that the root cause of the issue has been a misunderstanding that stems from the nature of autism. Either a child has expressed something literally which has been interpreted incorrectly by (for example) a teacher, or a professional has misunderstood the autistic parent's form of communication and/or behaviour. This may occur because of child protection awareness material which confuses symptoms of abuse with facets of autism (e.g. lack of eye contact), and possibly because psychotherapeutic training doesn't tend to include autism awareness.

I am unaware of any evidence that wrongful accusations in this respect are more or less common than within the PNT population, but I am very aware that thanks to a lack of understanding of autism the issues may continue or even escalate. It is essential for the professional world to understand that autistic parents are highly likely to communicate in ways that are different from those the professional is used to, and that their way of interacting with professionals may cause questions to be raised. *But* those questions must be understood within the context of autism, otherwise mistakes may be made.

Another aspect of the issue that needs consideration is when both parent and child are autistic. While it may appear from a PNT perspective that the relationship is highly unusual, it may be the case that the parents are successfully meeting their autistic child's needs in the most autism-friendly manner imaginable.

Understanding what to teach

Autistic adults will often feel that they 'miss out' on a host of information that their PNT counterparts are familiar with, and therefore may worry that their lack of understanding – for example of PNT social interaction – might mean their child will suffer. However, I think that the opposite is sometimes the case. So many autistic parents take their role so seriously that the research they do into being the best possible parent in the world means that they become excellent parents. As anyone will tell you, having their child as a special interest can be hugely rewarding!

Knowing your child

If you are an autistic parent there is a much higher chance that you will have an autistic child. This can be a blessing, or it can be problematic. As you know, you may have very strong feelings about all sorts of things, and it may be the case that your child has equally strong feelings. But they may not be the same as yours, which can cause conflict. However, I do think that it's more likely that being the autistic parent of an autistic child will be of benefit – sometimes, to both of you. Being able to share the experiences of being autistic, having a degree of intuitive empathy that might otherwise be lacking, and, for some, just sharing so much time with another autistic person, can all be wonderful things.

Knowing your partner

Raising a child together with another parent means that the autistic parent needs to recognize that – irrespective of whether both parents are autistic or whether it's an autistic/PNT relationship – his partner may have views on parenting that differ from his own. Compromise for someone who has very strong views might feel unnatural and 'wrong', but as there seems to be no right or wrong way to carry out many aspects of parenting it's worth working out with a partner how parenting decisions are going to be made from an early stage.

When it comes to parenting, being autistic doesn't automatically mean anything

Lastly, a reminder. As in all other areas of life, being autistic does not dictate anything when it comes to parenting. No one has the right to assume anything in terms of your ability to parent based purely on an identification of autism. No one knows what kind of parent you will be, and no one can predict how being a parent will affect you. Being autistic cannot, in itself, tell anyone anything about your parenting skill set.

11

Contact with the criminal justice system

There is no agreed consensus as to whether autistic adults are either more or less likely to break the law than the PNT. On one hand, the general liking for and adherence to rules might suggest that an autistic individual is less likely to break the law. However, there are also compelling arguments as to why autistic adults might be more likely to fall foul of the law. In terms of following the rules, yes – many autistic adults like rules and will follow them, sometimes quite strictly. But individuals can only follow the rules if they actually know what they are – and not many people learn all the rules that their country call laws.

For many of the PNT, their understanding of the law stems not from a study of the law itself, but from a sense of what society will consider 'right' and 'wrong'. There are some laws that most people are highly aware of (e.g. wearing a seatbelt), but the vast majority are almost inherently 'understood'. This may put an autistic individual at a huge disadvantage; he may not have the same inherent understanding of what is deemed 'right' (lawful) and 'wrong' (unlawful), as his understanding of right and wrong relate to ethical and moral issues rather than the law.

What is absolutely clear is that one can, of course, be autistic and undeniably criminal at the same time – by which I mean that if one is fully aware that one is breaking the law, there is intent to do so, and one understands the implications. However, it is equally clear – to me, at least – that some autistic people who break the law do so in a manner more closely related to autism than to criminal intent. This is where things get very tricky. Being autistic does not in itself 'excuse' anyone from law-breaking – but, at the same time, it can give us a rather different perspective on why a law may have been broken.

Some issues relating to the law which may cause autistic people difficulty include:

Trust

If an adult trusts others he may simply believe what they say when they coerce him into breaking the law. People who don't have any significant understanding of autism may find this hard to comprehend. The difficulty in correlating a high level of intellectual and verbal ability with a profound lack of understanding of who is trustworthy may be a step too far for some. And yet it is clear that there are some adults who simply will believe people without question when they are told something. This can lead to criminal activity on the part of the autistic person – as a direct result of coercion or manipulation by an unethical 'other'.

Lack of intent

Some autistic individuals who engage in criminal activity do so with entirely different intentions – almost as if the actual breaking of the law has not even occurred to them. For example, pursuing a passionate interest may mean that the person breaks a law along the way; perhaps hacking is an obvious example of this. In pursuit of knowledge an autistic adult may carry out unlawful hacking – but if she knows that she is not doing so for unlawful gain it may be that she simply does not think of the act as criminal, even though it is.

Lack of understanding of cause and effect

If one does not have a clear understanding of cause and effect it may be that a crime can be committed without realizing it. Similarly, if one does not have the cognitive ability to 'see the bigger picture', one might act in a criminal manner without understanding that this is the case. In some cases of stalking, for example, the autistic adult appears genuinely to believe that he is behaving in a friendly (albeit intense) manner, with no understanding of the impact of his actions on the other person.

Lack of cross-neurological theory of mind

The lack of an intuitive empathic understanding of others' thoughts and feelings causes problems for some people. The inability to read body language, for example, may cause a person to misread a situation in a way that could subsequently result in a physical confrontation.

Meltdowns

Many autistic adults who suffer from meltdowns will report that they are literally unable to control their actions at the time. If the behaviour includes hitting, for example, it may be that there is no difference at the time between hitting oneself, the wall or others – which has obvious problematic connotations.

Dealing with the authorities

There are publications available in which you can read more on how being autistic might affect any contact with the criminal justice system, but over and above that, some points for both the autistic adult and the police to take into account include:

Identify yourself

It is essential that you alert the police that you are autistic at the first possible opportunity. The police (and other personnel) cannot be expected to know unless you tell them. Once they do know, then they must make reasonable adjustments to ensure you're not discriminated against.

Alert cards

You can get hold of alert cards that can assist in the above identification. In addition to the alert card it's useful to have a synopsis of the key things you would want the police to know in the unfortunate instance that you are arrested. Having these written down is infinitely more useful than relying on yourself to remember them when you are in a stressful situation.

An appropriate adult or advocate

However intellectually able you are, it is useful to have someone with you when you are being questioned. It may be that some interpretation of the questions is necessary to ensure that misunderstandings are avoided.

12

Celebrating autism

This last chapter, of course, doesn't apply to all autistic individuals – but it's about time that we started to acknowledge some of the wonderful characteristics that so many autistic children and adults give to the world. Some may be pretty obvious, others less so – but all are worthy of consideration. And of course, many or all of these qualities can be found in any population – but I do think that making the effort to counterbalance some traditional thoughts on how autism presents can be a necessary component in breaking down misconceptions and reducing unfair stereotypes. Finally, some of the following are suggestions or hypotheses rather than 'fact' – you can make up your own mind in terms of how far you buy into them . . .

Sense of humour

Whoever decided, long ago, that autistic people lack a sense of humour was clearly about as incorrect as a human being can be when understanding a population. For example, Sarah Hendrickx is not only a prolific autistic writer but has dabbled in being a stand-up comic! And you only need to start following a handful of autistic folk on Twitter to realize that their humour is evident all over the internet. I adore the humour I come across – usually on a daily basis – with my range of autistic friends and acquaintances. It's uplifting and powerful. Much of the humour is self-deprecating, and perhaps this might go some way towards dispelling another myth – that autistic people are egotistical.

Lack of ego

Contrary to what some people believe, many autistic individuals are almost totally lacking in ego. Many of the autistic adults I know are the first to put others' needs before their own, and in fact lack any kind of understanding as to how and why anyone could or would be egotistical. The concept of self-importance appears to me to be lacking in many autistic individuals; conversely, many autistic adults will put others' happiness and needs well before their own in importance and value. This can cause problems, but must surely be recognized, and valued as an extraordinary individual characteristic.

Honesty

Some might label this quality as being 'too direct', 'blunt', 'literal'. I call it being honest. Quite simply, if you really want to know the truth about something, ask your autistic friend. It's far more likely that you'll get an honest answer than anything embellished, or hidden under a cloak of social nicety. If you really want to know the answer to whether it's noticeable that you've put on weight, you know who to ask . . .

Lack of adherence to nonsensical rules

This is another one that can get autistic people into trouble – and yet to me it's admirable in the extreme! The ability, in the name of honesty and truthfulness, to ignore social hierarchy or unwritten convention that makes no logical (autistic) sense should surely be celebrated. While perhaps socially unconventional, the child who kindly corrects her teacher who has got something wrong in her lesson, or the office worker who contacts his chief executive to point out a spelling mistake in her email, are demonstrating the level of equality that so many autistic people have. They so often simply see people as genuinely equal, and refuse to acknowledge socially constructed hierarchies of importance.

Degree of passion

Again, this is so often seen as a negative – 'obsessive behaviour'. And yet the passionate interests of many autistic people should surely be celebrated. Definitions of challenging behaviour refer to levels of intensity, duration and frequency – all which can be found in some people's engagement with their subject of interest – but this cannot always be seen as a negative. Having a passionate interest in something can be amazing for the individual – and it has a massive contribution to make to the wider society. After all, advances in academic disciplines, among others, may well stem from autistic passion . . .

World-changing ideas

It's worth contemplating just how many breakthrough moments in history may have had their origins in autistic thinking. The way in which the autistic brain works, the 'different' way of processing information, the ability to think 'outside the box' – it's certainly possible (even probable) that these cognitive capabilities can lead to dramatic changes in all sorts of areas that subsequently impact on the world. Information technology is perhaps one of the most obvious recent examples in which one might consider autistic thinking as having a powerful influence, but throughout history it would be fascinating to consider positive autistic influences in a range of areas, including academia, science, electronics, mechanics and the arts.

What you see is what you get

I don't necessarily mean this literally (see the next paragraph), but in terms of honesty and the lack of a hidden agenda I do think many autistic adults are very straightforward and don't play the sorts of 'social games' that can sometimes be found within the PNT population.

What you see is not what you get

Not that I really need to mention it again, but of course, taking into account all the masking and internalizing I've already written about, it's highly advisable not to make any assumptions about an autistic person based on outward appearances. Always remember, autism is in the brain – and unless you can magically see into someone's brain and experience their experiences, you don't automatically know what's going on in there.

Lack of interest in being 'top dog'

So many autistic adults want to do the best they can in particular areas, be it an interest, a job or a relationship – but the point is that this drive to want to do the best they can is just that. It's not a search for recognition, awards or prizes – it's simply the desire to do the best they can for their own peace of mind and satisfaction. Very often those same individuals are the ones who strive to remain 'invisible'. They don't want recognition or acknowledgement, as that level of exposure can be anxiety-inducing in the extreme; they may be happiest contributing magnificently to society in their own quiet, unobtrusive manner.

Trustworthiness

Plenty of autistic people are incredibly trustworthy. Literally, say the word and it's 'job done'. They can make the most amazing employees, friends, partners, buddies . . . if they say it's going to be done, you can rely on the fact that it will. No excuses, no missed deadlines, no half measures. Similarly, there may be no false emotions in a relationship (of any kind), no lies (white ones or otherwise), and a level of honesty that can be refreshing indeed.

Level of logic

Autistic people make a whole lot of sense – when one understands the world from their perspective. I am less convinced that the PNT actually makes as much logical sense. Having an autistic person explain her thinking from an individual perspective can be an extraordinary experience – illuminating, fascinating, eye-opening.

Accepting

I find that many autistic adults are remarkably non-judgemental and accepting of difference in all kinds of ways. It's very rare to find an autistic person who is discriminatory in terms of gender, sexuality, physicality, appearance, disability, fashion, style, age – in fact, in any imaginable way. I suspect that such differences simply do not appear on the autistic radar, such is the illogicality of discrimination.

Problem solving

If there is a problem, sometimes an excellent way of getting it solved is to ask an autistic person for her view. So often, she will see the problem in a different way from others and, therefore, be able to supply a solution that others have been unable to identify. Sometimes those solutions may be unorthodox – but they may well work!

Highly evolved principles

Another aspect that can get autistic people into trouble – and yet this ability not to 'go with the flow' if the autistic person has standards and principles that are against the grain can be of exceptional value. The autistic person who raises issues that others don't can play a hugely beneficial role in society.

Some see being autistic as a blessing, some see it as a curse. Everyone has their own thoughts and feelings on the subject. But my life has been made extraordinarily rich as a direct result of the autistic people within it, for which I will be for ever grateful.

I genuinely hope you've enjoyed reading this book.

Index